IN CELEBRATION OF A
Legacy

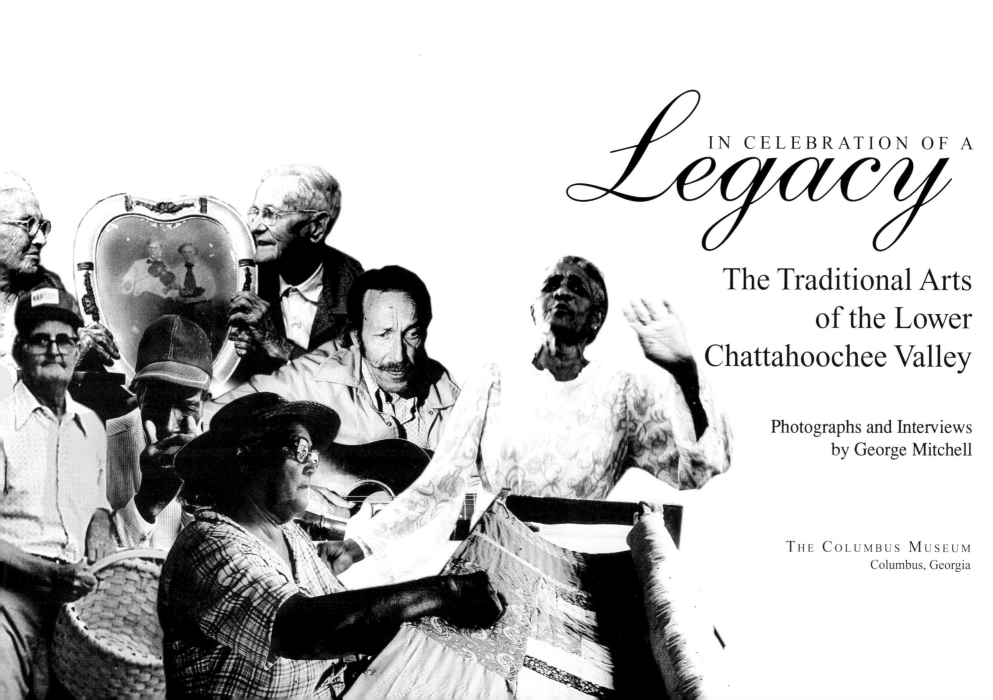

In Celebration of a
Legacy

The Traditional Arts
of the Lower
Chattahoochee Valley

Photographs and Interviews
by George Mitchell

THE COLUMBUS MUSEUM
Columbus, Georgia

Revised printing 1998 by the Historic Chattahoochee Commission with permission from The Columbus Museum, Inc.

Grant assistance provided by the Georgia Council for the Arts, Alabama State Council on the Arts, and the Friends of the "Ma" Rainey Blues Museum, Inc.

Manufactured in the United States of America

For more *information about this book, or other or other publications sponsored by the Historic Chattahoochee Commission, contact:*

Historic Chattahoochee Commission
Post Office Box 33
Eufaula, AL 36072-0033
E-mail: hccl@zebra.net
www.hcc-al-ga.org
(334) 687-9755

or

Post Office Box 942
LaGrange, GA 30241
(706) 845-8440

Library of Congress Cataloging-in-Publication Data

Mitchell, George, 1944-
    In celebration of a legacy : the traditional arts of the Lower Chattahoochee Valley
photographs and interviews by George Mitchell;
foreword by Fred Fussell.
        p.   cm.
    ISBN 0-945477-12-0 (pbk. : acid-free)
    1. Ethnic arts—Chattahoochee River Valley. I. Title.
NX506.M58   1998
700'.9758—dc21   98-12362
                                                                         CIP

ACKNOWLEDGEMENTS

This book is one of four elements which, together, comprise the project entitled "In Celebration of a Legacy: The Traditional Arts of the Lower Chattahoochee River Valley." The other elements are a record album of music which is traditional to the region, a Folk Festival of the Chattahoochee Valley and an exhibition of objects, both old and contemporary, which demonstrated the innate creativity of the region's traditional peoples.

Primary support for this project was provided from three sources; the Columbus Museum of Arts and Sciences, Inc., Columbus, Georgia; The Historic Chattahoochee Commission, Eufaula, Alabama; and the National Endowment for the Arts, Folk Arts Division, Washington, D.C.

The idea and plan for this work was developed by Fred C. Fussell, Curator of the Columbus Museum of Arts and Sciences and the majority of the fieldwork, photography, tape recordings, and general execution of the project was conducted by George Mitchell, Project Folklorist.

Thanks are due to William Scheele, Director of the Columbus Museum, for his initial encouragement in developing the project and for his continual interest and encouragement as the project progressed.

The following people served as consultants:

John Burrison, Professor of Folklore, Georgia State University
John Lupold, Assistant Professor of History, Columbus College
Elaine Thomas, Head, Art Department, Tuskegee Institute
Douglas Purcell, Director, Historic Chattahoochee Commission
Frank T. Schnell, Curator of Ethnology and Anthropology, Columbus Museum

To them we are grateful for their willingness to share their expertise and knowledge concerning the traditions of the region and its culture.

Special thanks are due to Kathy Casleton, Museum secretary, who patiently transcribed, typed and retyped the many hours of taped interviews from which the text of this book is drawn.

Sam Mitchell, a journalism student at Georgia State University, served diligently as field research assistant during the summer of 1980.

Marilyn Lee worked against the clock to complete the mechanical art for this book.

The American Folklife Center at the Library of Congress most kindly loaned recording equipment as did the Georgia Folklore Society.

Henry Willet, folklorist for the Alabama State Council on the Arts & Humanities, was very helpful in providing encouragement and leads during the course of field research.

Literally hundreds of citizens of the Chattahoochee Valley were helpful in providing leads, directions to the whereabouts of informants, and other information regarding traditional life in the region.

And finally, the most special thanks of all are due to those kind people who allowed us to go into their homes, their shops and into their backyards to photograph and record and who were willing to share with us their treasured possessions.

A NOTE FROM THE HISTORIC CHATTAHOOCHEE COMMISSION

In 1981 the Historic Chattahoochee Commission (HCC) and the National Endowment for the Arts helped to underwrite printing costs associated with The Columbus Museum's *In Celebration of a Legacy: Traditional Arts of the Chattahoochee Valley* publication. This book and its companion compact disc of folklife and traditional music is now being re-released under the sponsorship of the Historic Chattahoochee Commission with grant assistance provided by the Georgia Council for the Arts, Alabama State Council on the Arts, and the Friends of the "Ma" Rainey Blues Museum, Inc. The timelessness of George Mitchell's photographs and his field recordings is attested to by the continuing strong interest in folkways in both Alabama and Georgia as well as other parts of the country. The pioneer in this effort in the Chattahoochee Valley is HCC staff folklorist, Fred Fussell. In 1979 Mr. Fussell conceived the idea for this book as well as the very successful "Chattahoochee Folk Festival" which ran for five years. During his years as a curator at The Columbus Museum he continued his focus on folklife research and activities in this region. In 1996 he curated the exhibition, "In Our Own Backyard: The Folk Art and Traditional Expressions of the Chattahoochee Valley." The exhibition has received positive reviews at The Columbus Museum and the Wiregrass Museum of Art. Mr. Fussell writes a quarterly "Chattahoochee Folkways" column for the HCC's *Chattahoochee Tracings* newsletter and is busy working on a new book tentatively entitled "Folklife in the Chattahoochee Valley." All of these projects are being sponsored under the auspices of the HCC's ongoing Chattahoochee Valley Folklife Project.

We hope that a new generation of folklife enthusiasts will enjoy reading this book, viewing George Mitchell's photographs, and listening to his field recordings from almost twenty years ago. The work of recording this region's varied folkways will continue under the direction of Mr. Fussell as the HCC seeks ways to stimulate renewed interest in this often-neglected phase of our cultural development. Time is of the essence as many traditional artisans and musicians have already passed away. Their unique ways of expressing themselves would be forever lost without an ongoing program to record their music, photograph their handiwork, and research the cultural influences that shaped the creative minds of these people. It is a mission too important to overlook in an era where technology is obliterating our former way of doing things.

The HCC joins with The Columbus Museum, and other organizations who provided grant assistance, in making this second printing of "In Celebration of a Legacy" available to the general public and folk historians. We are also proud of the companion traditional music compact disc and trust that it will provide many hours of listening pleasure to folk music fans.

Douglas C. Purcell
Executive Director
Historic Chattahoochee Commission

A NOTE FROM THE COLUMBUS MUSEUM

In 1981, the then-Columbus Museum of Arts and Sciences published *In Celebration of a Legacy: The Traditional Arts of the Lower Chattahoochee Valley* with the assistance of the Historic Chattahoochee Commission and the National Endowment for the Arts. Much more than a vanity publication, this text was a component of a larger *fête galanté* which featured a major multi-media exhibition, a live arts festival and a musical recording.

The curator-in-charge, Fred Fussell, worked with folklorist George Mitchell to seek out the finest of our region's traditional artists and make a lasting record of their particular specialties. The book was the visual record for the artists and the vinyl LP record documented the musicians' products. For the Museum it was a definitive announcement to the larger museum community that Columbus was sincere in its efforts to collect the work of its native artists. For the broader public, it was the opportunity to have an in-depth introduction to those forms of folk art which are largely handed down from generation to generation through oral traditions or through ongoing apprenticeship.

Seventeen years later, the role of folk art in mainstream American museums is unquestioned in its validity. The Columbus Museum now has significant holdings in traditional or native arts, and its cultural neighbor to the north in Atlanta, the High Museum of Art, is the first art museum in the nation to establish a curatorial position in folk art. The American Folk Art Museum in New York has given high visibility to this time-honored approach to creativity. Collectors now rush to seek out such artists, and we all respect the immense talents of our own backyard personalities in a manner they deserve. But the world is much smaller, and there are more similarities between Columbus, Ohio and Columbus, Georgia than one might expect. More than ever we need to protect and preserve what makes us unique. This recognition of our indigenous artists is an important step.

Therefore, it is with a great deal of pleasure and anticipation that we are able to re-issue that catalogue and to offer the music in a more contemporary form of digital recording. What makes this particularly pleasing is that two of the original instigators and creative talents – Fred Fussell and Doug Purcell of the Historic Chattahoochee Commission– have been so integrally involved in the success of this project. These two special individuals have done more to secure and safeguard the traditional arts in the lower Chattahoochee Valley than anyone else, and we all owe them a huge debt of gratitude. The Historic Chattahoochee Commission has been a driving force in promoting such projects as this, and the native arts have continued to thrive because of them.

The importance of such documents as this publication or the recording becomes even more clear when we consider that several of the original artists in the project are no longer with us. This re-issuance of George Mitchell's field notes and the duplication of the original master tapes of the musical performances will assure that these artists' work live on for another generation to learn from and to enjoy. The Columbus Museum is proud to be able to partner again with the Historic Chattahoochee Commission and make this worthwhile project a reality.

Charles T. Butler
Director
Columbus Museum

FOREWORD

It was a warm November afternoon in 1968. Just a few days earlier the first killing frost of the season had browned the kudzu that I passed as I drove south on a country road from Lumpkin to the home of Lucius Robinson.

L.M. Moye, who owned the farm on which Lucius was a tenant, had told me that Luke had set aside this day for making sugar cane syrup, a task which he had done annually for many years.

Turning left onto a twin dirt trail, I cruised slowly, raising dust across the vast field of bare cotton stalks which surrounded Luke's place.

As I drove near, I could see his little white washed frame house with its screened porch, neatly trimmed privet shrubs, and clean swept yard. Brown snuff bottles with their necks buried in the sand lined frost-bitten flower beds. Worn tractor tires, painted white, stood on edge in a circular parade around the front yard.

Stopping beside the house near a pair of ramshackle pick-ups, I was promptly greeted by a half-dozen nervously friendly hounds, tails tucked.

I could barely discern the low silhouettes of Luke and another elderly man who sat beneath the pole shelter behind the house.

I got out and waved. Returning my wave, the two men stood to greet me.

Nearby, an old red horse mule, sweating in the sun, circled slowly as he pulled the long sweetgum sweep, oblivious of the fact that no one was feeding cane into the mill.

The late afternoon sun was dropping and the men had just filled the eighty gallon kettle with cane juice. A large supply of wood, the remnants of discarded fencing for the most part, was piled nearby for fuel. A slender line of brown smoke rose from the chimney of the furnace into the still autumn sky.

After sitting, we exchanged pleasantries concerning the weather and the crops. Soon, the conversation drifted into a discussion of the syrup-making process and of old times on the farm.

Lucius Robinson made syrup, not only for himself, but for his neighbors who grew sugar cane. He had done so for years, taking a portion of the sweet syrup from each cooking in exchange for his labor. This portion, or toll, he used for himself, sold, or more often gave away to friends.

As the sky darkened and the air began to chill, the two men slowly brought the dark juice to a simmer and then to a hard boil. As the juice boiled, pulp and other impurities which rose to the top were carefully skimmed away with a shallow punched-tin ladle. The rim of the kettle, six feet in diameter, was constantly dampened with a wet cloth to prevent scorching.

The men worked with a quiet determination broken only occasionally with jokes pertaining to Lumpkin gossip — an eternal pastime.

Hearing the slamming of car doors, we turned to view the arrival of a half-dozen neighbors who drifted slowly past the house to the shed where we sat.

As the evening grew darker, the hot fragrant juice slowly cooked thick and the crowd grew to twenty or more, sitting and standing around the furnace. Time passed and the tempo of the evening livened.

Dark faces, glowing in the firelight, showed white teeth and eyes as sweet potatoes were roasted in the ashes of the furnace and a bottle of corn whiskey was passed freely from hand to hand.

Someone — a young woman — began humming a hymn and the night was suddenly flooded with a strong harmony of voices in song

I sat still, intimidated by the sudden and unexpected power of the music which surrounded me. With uncanny spontaneity, one hymn sprang from another, accompanied by hand clapping and shouts. The sky was now completely dark and the flickering light of the furnace fire cast long shadows which danced strangely to the rhythm of the hands and voices around me.

"I'm ready when you call me, Lord, But won't you give me just a little more time?"

Remembering that refrain, repeated many times that evening, it seems especially meaningful to me now. That was twelve years ago, a short time. But now the old red mule is dead. Lucius Robinson has moved to another house. He no longer makes sugar cane syrup. Has grown too old, he says.

Time, for many such folkways of the people of the Chattahoochee Valley, has run out.

For the past eighteen months, beginning in April, 1980, the Columbus Museum of Arts and Sciences has supported an effort to recover as much as possible of the folk traditions of the region in which we live; the traditions expressed by the people of the Valley in their music, their work, their creativity, and their lives.

During this effort, George Mitchell, project folklorist, has traveled thousands of miles in the Valley area of Alabama and Georgia. He has contacted, interviewed, recorded, and photographed over three hundred people who are the primary bearers of knowledge pertaining to ways indigenous and traditional to this region of the Deep South.

Most of these people, like Lucius Robinson, are old timers. Modern communication methods, mass production of goods, and readily available transportation have caused recent generations to set aside the old ways. More than a dozen of the people contacted during this project have died in the past few months. Among them — Idus Freeman of Webster County, Georgia, who knew of old ways of working wood, steam railroads, and the chants used by crews in lining track; Henry Lee Thornton, a basket maker of the same county whose rich bass voice resounded with laughter through the pine woods; Henry Blankenship, also of Webster County, a master craftsman and musician. A man whose life was a pattern for others.

To do what George Mitchell has done here ten years hence seems unlikely.

But perhaps not; regional traditions die hard. The weather aside, it's still easy enough to tell, when you alight from an airplane, that you're in Columbus, Georgia, and not Columbus, Ohio. The two cities continue to maintain distinctively regional cultural attributes, as they should. Let's hope that we can keep those regional differences alive throughout this country, for a long time to come.

Fred C. Fussell
Project Director
September 19, 1981

PROJECT DIRECTOR UPDATE

When I wrote the above foreword to this book in 1981, only three years had passed since I had left the town of Lumpkin in rural Stewart County, Georgia, after living there for more than eight years. I had been literally and totally immersed during those years, every single day, in the traditional life of that small Southern community. My job as the director of crafts for a fledgling living history museum had positioned me to regularly associate with a group of remarkable traditional people whose general knowledge and life experiences were in many ways holdovers from a previous era. Yet, even though they were employed by the museum to portray the lifeways of an earlier time, and they themselves were of a culture which held as staunchly as it possibly could onto its deeply embedded social and communal traditions, they were not people of the past. They were very much citizens of this century.

Folklore is not history, and cultural traditions and the people who maintain them are not relics of the past. The traditional attributes of a region are constantly and forever changing, continually adjusting to the conditions of the times and in response to the demands of necessity. It's the same here and everywhere. "The past isn't over," wrote William Faulkner, "it isn't even past!"

The words you read here and the likenesses you see here and the voices you hear here are simple documents of living traditions that have continued unabated in the Chattahoochee Valley from the past to the present. I now realize, as I perhaps did not in 1981, that our traditions are not likely to diminish, or to end, or to disappear. Now I realize that they will fittingly change from what they were into what they will become.

As this century draws to a close, we celebrate the rich cultural legacy that we have so fortunately inherited from the past. We should also equally celebrate the opportune promise of the cultural riches that lie ahead of us, so firmly founded upon the legacy of the present.

Fred C. Fussell
June 24, 1998

IN CELEBRATION OF A

Legacy

Barbour County, Alabama

William Grant blowing the harp, Russell County, Alabama

Bessie and W. E. Hannah, Russell County, Alabama

Whitewash on trees and rocks, Early County, Georgia

Bessie Thornton, Talbot County, Georgia

BESSIE THORNTON

Bessie Thornton was born in the last year of the 19th century in Thomaston, Georgia, and moved to her present home of Talbot County, Georgia, when she was in her twenties. At the age of 82, she still makes a couple of quilts a month. Her needlework is well-known around the small town of Woodland and whites in the area buy her quilts almost as fast as she can make them.

We were raised on a farm. Lord, you raised some of everything. It ain't like it is now. They ain't farming now like they used to. We were more healthy then. Since they stopped raising chickens and hogs and things like they ought to, and instead go out and buy this stuff out of the storehouse, we more sickly. That was fresh we was eating off the yard. Daddy didn't have to buy nothing but some sugar. He carried corn to the mill, he have fields of wheat and carry that stuff to the mill and make bread. We didn't go to the storehouse and buy everything like you buy now. Folks have done got too rich.

We didn't come like y'all come now. We come up bare-footed. Now we had plenty of old brogans with these here tacks in the side of 'em. You had plenty shoes like that, but, honey, you wash your foots and legs and went to Sunday school barefooted. I washed for the hands that Papa had hired plowing to get the money to get me a pair of slippers to wear when I got married.

Now, you had to have you some age to court around. Papa wouldn't allow us no courting till we got to be something old. You had to get a certain age before a boy could go with you anywhere and they gave you strict hours. We didn't know like children know now. I wasn't raised like these folks now raised. If a girl come up wrong, we didn't know it. Our parents told us, you musn't go with her no more, say, she grown. You were left a fool in that way. You didn't read all this stuff and see all these things over the TV. Now, I just sit and look and study and think. I wonders many a time what gonna be next.

Peoples is raising their children now for the chain gang. A lot of little children this day and time, when you eat dinner, tell you quick, "I want that piece right there," the best piece in the dish. Well, it wasn't all such as that. Mama and Papa ate first. They sit down and eat, and then fix these children's plate and don't hear a mouth, don't hear nary one crying. You don't find that now.

Everybody whipped the children back then, not just the mama and the daddy. But you hit a child now, you hear the parents talking about I got a knife and I'm gonna cut that woman or man, better not hit my child. Everybody whipped me. You wouldn't tell the truth, somebody gonna whip you. I thought Mrs. Allie Taylor and a bunch of 'em was kin to us, and come to find out they ain't a bit of kin. You don't find that this day and time, man. You didn't hear tell of much you hear tell of now. Lord, these folks living too fast, living too fast.

There was more children raised then. We had a better time, we were more together. People would help people when they got sick. Mama would get us to come in from the field, say, "Jane over yonder sick, carry this dinner over there to her. I'm going over there tomorrow to cook dinner, wash her clothes and hang 'em up." Well, people's done got above that now. You could die, unless'n you do what they

want, go their way, drink liquor and do everything they do. They ain't gonna pay you no attention; man, you just somewhere sitting in the world. Since my husband died 24 years ago, I've had one mess of sausage and a little piece of backbone give to me. These folks will kill a hog week before Christmas, they'll kill him at night, dry it up at night, ain't gonna give you a cracklin to make you hoe cake of bread. But, if you shut your hand up, nothing'll ever get in there. I keep mine open.

Papa didn't hire out nary one of us. He say he didn't have nar a child he'd hire to nobody, he always raised a plenty and worked us at home. I wasn't hired out until I was grown and married. Then I hired myself out, first hiring out that I ever done. I worked for one family, for Mr. Mill's family, for 30 years, from 1928 to 1957. I went to nurse with Miss Emma, Mr. Mills' wife's mother — she died two days short of being 104 years old. And when I first started I was washing her and combing her hair and dressing her in the morning. I did that for a month or more. Then they wanted me in the kitchen. Well, I went to keeping house until death for all of 'em. I got paid a dollar a week.

I got paid a dollar a week till they got sick. They went up on me then. I worked day and night then. But they did not give me 50 and 60 dollars a week like they did this white nurse. She would say, "Bessie, you're a good nurse, come here and let me show you something. Look at me fix the bed just like it ought to be and dress Miss Liz Mae like it ought to be," and I said, "I don't need no showing, I already know." I said I could lift Miss Liz Mae without her hollering and screaming and she couldn't do it. And then I heard Mr. Mills tell her one day that she didn't do nothing but sit down and call me all the time, that Miss Liz Mae wanted me to stay with her and she could go home. And then they didn't give me half what they give her. I resented it a heap, but I had to work right on. When you ain't got nothing and don't want to steal, you want to live right and do right, you'll work harder than ever to hold your name.

I told Mr. Mills one day, "Mister, all of 'em done moved off the place and left you. If you want me to stay, you got to give me a home so when I get old I will have somewhere to sit down if nothing else." And he did do that after Miss Liz Mae died.

Love is a funny thing. And I know what love was one time, 'cause when my husband died, I lost it. My first husband got to running around with other women and it tore things up. Y'all got to pull together and stick together, or it won't last. Well, I didn't love Jimmy, my second husband, when I married him. But I said, Well, I don't want to live all my life by myself, and while I'm young I should have some company when I go home, have somebody to say something to me. You marry a man and don't love him, if he be good to you and you be good to him, you come to love that person. I done been through with it, I know what I'm talking about. That's the reason I'm so satisfied now. I don't never expect to marry no more. I don't want nobody else.

I had five children. I've done lived to see 'em all be grown, married, and all of 'em done died except two. My baby boy, my Jimmy — he was born and raised here — he got to running around here with these boys, he got to drinking and I couldn't do nothing with him. I told him more times than I got fingers and toes, "Honey, you killing yourself." I fussed and I quarreled and I told him he couldn't do it here in the house with me. But when he married and got out, he did just what he see the rest of the folks do. He's covered up and can't say a word today and I'm sitting here, ain't I? This fast life will hurry you away from here. There's more in taking care of yourself instead of living so fast. I do believe if I'd been like some women I see, I'd been dead and gone. And I know some women come along when I did, they look so bad it's pitiful. As I tell them, I know I ain't pretty — I ain't never thought I was pretty — but I know I pass, 'cause I believe in taking care of myself.

I started making quilts as a child. Anything I wanted to do, I got up and done it. The first one I ever made was back yonder when you couldn't get nothing to make a quilt out of but a old apron or pieces of an old dress. Well, my grandma made quilts. Everything I see my grandma do, I gotta do it too. My grandma would cut square blocks, and the first one I sewed together, she said that's wrong. I had it every whichaway, I didn't have sense enough to run a straight line. So she pulled it out twice on me. I never will forget it; I was only 10 years old, sitting down by a big hickory fire. I sat there that night and she showed me how to piece a quilt. "You don't take them long stitches; take the little bitty stitches." I made four or five blocks that night.

So I decided to make a whole quilt and surprise her. She be busy working, I'd steal and go out behind the house and I pieced that whole quilt. Grandma had a fit, and she told Mama that I be the onliest girl in the family that have patience to do like she did. And Grandma had a whole lot of

Henry County, Alabama

strings, and I got them strings and I sat down and made a string quilt. And I've made hundreds of quilts since. I got quilts all over the world, every whichaway. I've cut up more cloth than nary any woman in the United States. I'm about the onliest one in this area, in Talbot County, that sit down and piece a quilt. Can't find nobody else around here that do it. They're too lazy, ain't got time.

When I was doing housework for the white folks, I come home and cook supper, feed 'em, wash up my dishes, bathe my children, put 'em in the bed, and my husband go to bed. "You come to bed," he say, "I know you ain't gonna sew tonight." I said, "You just go on and get in bed." Didn't know anything and it'd be twelve, one o'clock I be sitting here piecing on my pieces.

One time I hadn't pieced but one block on a quilt, and my husband said, "Nobody ever get that but me." It was my husband's quilt. He was really proud and loved to sleep under it. Mrs. Booth, this white woman, say that was the prettiest quilt she ever saw in her life. She had a mortal fit, and she had to have it. She offered my husband all kind of money for it, but he wouldn't take it. He slept under it till he died.

Henry County, Alabama

Growing Martin houses, Quitman County, Georgia

Lonzie Thomas, Lee County, Alabama

Marion County, Georgia

Marion County, Georgia

ROBERT SAXON

Columbus, Georgia, had a very active country music scene in the 1920's, 1930's and 1940's, with numerous local live radio programs and stage shows devoted to it. Robert Saxon was one of the most popular of the city's country musicians during that period, playing almost every stringed instrument and the piano, depending on what the group needed. At the age of 70, he is still a superb country singer and piano player.

My pappy did some of everything. Farmed, worked in the mills, made moonshine. He'd just quit one job and go to making moonshine. Quit moonshining and go back to another job. He made it and sold it. Got caught once or twice. He got locked up when he was living in Hall County, Georgia, got out on bail, and he went scouting — what he called scouting — in the mountains. He scouted for six months. And then one night he come in at one o'clock, gonna get him something to eat. My mother, she always kept supper ready for him in case he come, but he hadn't come in months. That particular time she had boiled chicken and dumplings, and he come in and sit down, and he ain't no sooner sit down when here come footsteps on the porch, a knock on the door. They caught him and put him back in jail.

We was poor. We was so poor we wouldn't hardly make a shadow. That was when you were poor enough to have to wear your daddy's long old gingham shirt, and that's all you had to wear. We couldn't even buy me a pair of overalls. Sometimes I would lose two days meals out of three. Didn't have nothing to eat. My mother — she had ten of us, and they was little bitty ones — she'd get us up at four o'clock in the morning, carry us way up the road three or four miles, pick cotton for somebody. We would make enough to get a few meals.

We could have got straightened up a little, but my ma was a stinker about whiskey money; she didn't want no whiskey money. That was against her religion. And mine, too. Anybody say your daddy work selling whiskey, it gets to you after awhile. The only way she used any whiskey money was when Pap would go buy some groceries with it, and that's when we would have something to eat. Well, I'll tell you about Ma, anyone can tell you — white or colored — my ma was more than just a woman. She was a fighting woman. Pap, he was going hell western most of the time back in the hill country, and she had to keep ten younguns going.

Lots of time we'd eat possums. Possum is pretty good. A chicken 'bout as nasty as a possum. A chicken is a cannibal too. A chicken will eat anything you throw down there, he'll eat a dead possum even. But when you're in our country, you'll eat anything. We'd go possum hunting at night. Had dogs that would tree the possum. Shake him out the tree and let the dogs catch him, then make the dogs quit and not bite him. That old possum, rolled up, you'd catch him by the tail and carry him home. Put the possums in a pen and feed 'em apples that wasn't ripe, maybe some chestnuts, whatever. She'd feed 'em about two weeks, if we could wait that long. Well, it takes that thought away from 'em after awhile, you know, about what all kinds of dead animals and things they been gnawing on.

Robert Saxon, Muscogee County, Georgia

I been working in mills ever since I was about 11. Before I come to Columbus, we worked in mills in Atlanta, Macon, Forsyth, and some other places. Just moving about. Moved to Columbus when I was about 14. I started off picking up bobbins off the floor, old bobbins that run that thread in the spoolroom. Then I went to doffing. I doffed I reckon fifty years all total. In different mills — Bibb Mill, Columbus Mills and Swift.

The first instrument I started out on was a old pump organ. Pap had a little old bull, and a man wanted him bad, and said he'd trade him a pump organ for it, so Pap swapped him the bull for that pump organ. "Let old Robert learn how to play it." I never will foget how he said that. I was a little bitty old thing, couldn't even reach the pedals. My brother, he pumped it for me. I started playing piano when I was seven. I got to going to church, playing for brush arbors. I never will forget the last song I played on that old organ. I was at the store, and I heared that record about the "Wreck of the Old Ninety-Seven." And I sit till I got that thing in my mind. And when I got home, I went in there and went to playing that song on the pump organ. I also sang it in the childish way. And before I got through, they had that street flocked out there; the street done filled up. Everybody come up yonder, tell 'em you oughta go in there and hear him, stuff like that. And my daddy and all of 'em come home. They pulled that old pump organ out on the porch, and they started throwing pennies on the porch. I reckon that's the most fun in my life till I got to where I was 20, 25 years old.

The first Sunday morning I was in Columbus — we come in on a Tuesday — I was walking along Second Avenue and come to a church at 27th Street. I probably had holes in my pants from one end to the other. I was walking by that church and they was singing, and I couldn't hear no music, so I just turned around and went back and looked in. There wasn't nobody at the piano. So I went on in, sit down and played the piano, just made myself at home. I played piano for them I guess about ten months.

Wasn't long after that a deacon in a Baptist church on 20th Street in Phenix City got me and a guitar player to come over there and play in his church. We went in there and there's an old lady playing pretty nice, as church music goes. She was playing that old song "Have you been to Jesus," and she just getting it bump, bump, bump, not putting anything into it. When come our time to play, that tune the way she played it was still sticking in my mind. I wasn't intending to, but just unconsciously I just fell out on that song and put it in four fourth time, like I'm playing square dancing. I heard that old lady tell that preacher, "Don't you ever invite them here again." He said, "I didn't invite 'em here this time." And the deacon who invited us, he heard them talking, and he got up and announced, "Things are changing. These boys have never played in a Baptist church before. They have only played in Holiness churches. But things are changing." See, the music in Holiness Churches had more spirit to it. If you went into a Methodist or Baptist church and you went to revving things up a little bit, they'd ask you to go.

I started playing hillbilly music for money when I was about 15. My first job was right here in Columbus at the

water works. Used to be two houses down there, and they had square dances there. I think we made about half a dollar a piece playing for them square dances. Friday night and Saturday night. Later on, I played on a show with Uncle Bob — he was a black faced comedian, one of the world's best, a wiz dinger man. I worked in the mills and he hauled eggs and chickens in the daytime, and we played a show every night except Sunday. He preaching Sunday night. And I played on WRBL near about 50 years ago.

I played all kinds of instruments in these different groups. I never have kept a instrument two days that I didn't play something on it. I made a few instruments too. I made an axe handle fiddle. I got me one of these old-time record players, one of them you grind and turn, and took this round piece that's got the needle in it, and put it on the axe handle where the fiddle strings come at the bottom. And then I stuck this quart oil funnel into that thing that come off the record player. The sound come out of that, and you wouldn't believe it, you could hear that thing three blocks down the road. Music then didn't have amplifiers to back it up. The first time I tried it I was playing at a country show, and I was going to play the alto part with the fiddler on a good night waltz. And, man, when I cut down on that stinker, it just drowned the fiddle all to pieces. And one time I made a tenor banjo out of a two-gallon wesson oil can. And I put a fiddle neck on a mandolin and played it like a fiddle, called it the mandolin-fiddle. Never did make an instrument that didn't sell.

How do I think I got the gift? That's pretty hard to define. God knew what was going to happen before the foundation of the world. So, you see, there have been many a church that would never have had music if I hadn't played for them. So I just assume God gave me this ability to play enough for the members of the church to sing by. He figured maybe I'm gonna help him out in that way, undoubtedly because . . . There are things hard to explain unless you take

in the supernatural. And, oh well, when you get right down to it, the supernatural is the only thing we got when we name it, really.

You take me, when I was over there in the hospital, almost dead. Had a stroke in the face. This is hard for just anybody to believe, and I wouldn't blow up at nobody if they said they didn't believe it. But me, I know. My chest was swelled all the way up to my chin. I wasn't hardly breathing. I had to examine to see whether I was breathing. And the preacher walked off and left me. Later on, I asked him, "Why did you leave me, preacher?" He says, "I knew you were dying. I didn't want to see you die, Robert." But about the time he got out the door, a little youngun got up from the foot of the bed. Looked like a little girl, calico dress on, and hair down around her shoulders. She come around the foot of that bed and put her hands together and knelt down and started praying. And that whole room turned a copper light, just like somebody had turned on a copper light. The most beautiful light I've ever saw. I thought I was dying, and I folded my hands like you suppose to when you die I reckon. I figured I'm dying, there's nothing else I can do. And then the light turned back to normal. And I realized I'm breathing; I can see my chest going up and down, which it hadn't been. And I looked, and the little girl just faded away. And, man, I come out from under that stroke and recovered.

I believe I'm getting a little bit paid for what I did back in my young days. 'Cause I never turned a preacher down. If he needed a piano or organ player, I always played for him.

Cornshuck mop, Henry County, Alabama

Rev. George A. Moore, Talbot County, Georgia

Talbot County, Georgia

H. J. Niles' sugar cane mill, Russell County, Alabama

Sampling the cane juice

Barbour County, Alabama

ALICE HARRIS

Alice Harris was born near Camp Hill, Alabama, but moved to Columbus, Georgia, as a small child. She spent her teenage and adult years in Harris County, Meriweather County, and Atlanta, but moved back to Columbus about seven years ago. Once she mused, "My sisters have their children and grandchildren. Well, in my declining years, all I have is my dreams. And I put them into color and form." Her tiny apartment is full of her dreams pictured in bright colors on masonite boards. She writes poetry frequently and says all her poems are based on truth.

In reverence I stood gazing at a sunset one day. 'Twas in June on an evening quite fair. A prayer for forgiveness to my Maker I breathed for attempting this thing so rare.

Against the sunset I held a clear glass. On its surface my pigment I matched. From the blue of the sky and the gold of the sun some beauty was ultimately snatched.

Then I met an artist of the new school. He came from some country afar. He showed me a sketch which he called a duck but you would swear on your oath 'twas a star.

"Your art is old-fashioned, out-dated, antique. New abstract is taking the day. If you want to be famous, wealthy and smart, you should follow the trend all the way. Something to imagine, you see, should be left — not too obvious and finished," quoth he. He showed me another sketch he called a horse, but it looked like a donkey to me.

"If these are the things you have gathered, my friend, in your travel and study abroad, then down to earth and nature I'd stay with things simple, reminiscent of God. The hills are old-fashioned, so is the moon. The stars are old-fashioned too. Much that is old-fashioned, dearest and best has proven to be tried and true."

My paintings I do like the poetry I write, irrespective of fashion or creed. With my brush in sheer joy I fashion each stroke. Earth is filled with the lessons I need.

As the writer of music expresses his thoughts in tones that are sweet to the ear, so the writer of poetry a word picture wrought — great poems old-fashioned but dear.

In the quietness of dawn the clear notes of a bird stirred the soul of the writer of songs. On such things as this, inspiration is born to gladden the hearts of the throngs.

So the artist, with brushes, seeks to express, in loveliest color and form, the things he feels but cannot express when his soul with emotion is torn.

Alice Harris, Muscogee County, Georgia

Johnnie Ree Jackson, Talbot County, Georgia

JOHNNIE REE JACKSON

Johnnie Ree Jackson has lived in Talbot County, Georgia, since her birth in 1904. She spends most of her time making things. She makes especially good use of the pine tree; she uses the needles (or straw) for making baskets, hats, and saucers, and the burrs from the cones for making vases ranging in height from three inches to four feet. She utilizes corn shucks for making mats, hats, and chair bottoms. And, of course, she quilts.

My daddy owned his own farm. Him and my mama, both of 'em worked. Both of 'em just worked together. You know how they worked back then. Just like slavery nearly. And all six of us children worked. We didn't sit down and get to no shade like other folks. I done come up the rough way, mister. But we didn't mind working. It was just in us, I reckon.

I'm marked with my mama's mother. Birthmarked. I'm birthmarked in my left eye; can't hardly see nothing out of it. And we didn't even know I was marked until I was half grown. We was in the field one day and I covered up my right eye and I couldn't hardly see the cows. I said, "Mom, if I cover my right eye up I can't see at all." She reeled around in the field, said, "What you say, gal?" I say, "I just thought everybody was like that." She say, "I marked you with my mother." She marked me, but she didn't know it.

See, you can mark your children by doing something when you carrying 'em in your womb. Well, my mother was carrying me, and her mama — she was a Black Hawk Indian — she passed. She was dead, and they had her laying out on a plank in the house. You know, they laid 'em out in the cool and covered 'em up; they didn't have places to undertake and embalm. My mama went to look at her mother, but her stepfather said, "If I was you, Susie, I wouldn't look at her, 'cause she in bad shape." She had swelled up and everything. But my mama zurned her over her left shoulder; you know, didn't look at her straight, just glanced at her over her shoulder. And she was lying there, one eye open and the other shut. And by looking at her, she marked me. She always wondered was I marked.

People really do get marked. Now, I had a sister, she was picking muscadines, she got lots of 'em. But there was a special one at the top of the tree that she really wanted but she couldn't get it. Well, there was a bunch of muscadines on the neck of that baby she was pregnant with. Now I got a son here with a link of sausage on his hip, a mark look like sausage. When I was carrying him, one time I got all kind of sausage, but I didn't get the kind I wanted. And it sure on his hip.

The first thing I made when I was a child was these pine cone vases; glue pine burrs on these cotton spools and things. That was my first step, and then I just learned one thing from another. I could sew and I could do some of everything. Piece quilts, make pine straw baskets and cups, take these acorn squashes and make ashtrays out of 'em. I could do anything I wanted — bottom chairs, stuff squirrels and decorate 'em with pine buds, acorns, these July flies that shed and leave their shells, watermelon seeds, little old snail shells. I did needlework, crocheting, making dresses out of these old-fashioned sheets. My mama said, "Well, Tump" — that's my nickname, Tump, "I can do a lot of things, but you done passed me by."

Well, after I got married I wasn't making so many things 'cause I was raising nine children and working in the fields all the time. But I had a nervous breakdown in 1950. I was standing up working when my nerves just popped like a dead spring. Oh, man, I was in a fix. I couldn't even get out the house. I was so poorly, I couldn't eat, I couldn't sleep, and my mind was nearly gone. My stomach just tremble like a leaf. Well, this went on about 20 years. Doctors couldn't do nothing. Well, I went back to making those things. That help you to keep busy. I went to work making one thing and then another when I detected it helped my nerves. And the people would tell me, "Johnnie Ree, making all that stuff would get on my nerves." I said, "Well, it helping mine." See, it keep that worry off your mind. I prayed and I done everything and I'm back where you see me today.

I ride by a trash pile, I see something in it, I get out and pick it up. I have in my mind what I'm gonna make out of it. I make these things in my spare time. I don't neglect my field work. I work at nighttime. Everybody gone to bed, I'm sitting up crocheting, piecing up quilts, doing something.

Early County, Georgia

Chambers County, Alabama

Russell County, Alabama

Henry County, Alabama

Blacksmith shop, Lee County, Alabama

Macon County, Alabama

Lucius Robinson, Stewart County, Georgia

LUCIUS ROBINSON

Lucius Robinson has lived in Stewart County, Georgia, all his life. He first made white oak baskets as a young man and still makes them occasionally when he can get the wood.

If I live to see the 27th day of October, I'll be 77. Eleven children, all them grown and out. So I've been right here, ain't never been out of this county to do nothing. Ain't never had no trouble with the law. I go under my own law. I didn't have anything to do with the other fellow's business. The scripture tells you when you find a fool, leave him a fool. I done got by this long and I ain't had no trouble.

Been on the farm all my days. My daddy raised me on the farm; after I was married I farmed; and I had 11 children and raised them on the farm. My daddy had a big old red mule he plowed, and he'd make cotton like I don't know what. He started us picking cotton with little old flour sacks. We'd have flour sacks full of cotton. I always had something to do when I was a child. Not like people now, where a child get grown before he learns anything. My daddy had jobs for us. When we were small, he kept hogs, cows and things, and they were roving; we didn't have no pastures. We had to see after them cows and hogs. Then he started us tending to the mules. Had to water them down at the spring. We were so little we couldn't hardly get on a mule, but we'd get on some way and ride anyway. Children now, they don't have nothing for 'em to do. They come in and turn that TV on to look at it. We didn't have anything like that.

When I was coming up, I made things to use on the farm and all. Axe handles, scouring mops, washboards, things like that. When I was a boy, that's the way I made money, where I could tote it in my pocket. I didn't have no vice to hold the wood when I made an axe handle, so I'd drill two pins in a tree and I'd put my wood between them, take my draw knife and get out there and make axe handles. I made me a chisel for the first washboard I ever made. I took me a piece of iron, whipped it out and sharpened it and beveled it off and put me a handle on it. Got out there and got all the planks I could find round my daddy's place and sat down and made me a rub board. I always made rub boards. On a Saturday — we never did hardly plow on Saturday — that's what I'd be doing. I'd have rub boards sitting all across the yard. Shuck mops — put the holes in there and put your shucks in it. Put a handle on it. Put you a little soapy water down, get on that floor with that mop, and that thing clean that floor like I don't know what.

A white fellow that was by here the other day wanted me to make him some axe handles. I told him if he'd bring me the wood I'd make 'em. I can't go get the wood like I used to, you know. When I was coming up, you could just go anywhere and get the wood. Get wood off of anybody's place anytime. But now you can't do it. They don't allow you to. Long back then we could just go to the woods and cut white oak and hickory, anything we'd want to make anything out of, off of most anybody's place. But it's got to where you can't do that now. That's how come I have to charge so much for a basket now. And it takes a long time, too, to get that wood and make the splits and make that basket. And now you can't get no good splitting wood like you use to. You used to could go to the woods and cut a white oak and it would split out as smooth as your hand. Nowadays, some of it you can start and it'll just eat away. Then you got to get down and scrape it and everything to try to get it passable.

I did all right farming 'cause I was raising my living. I was going to the mill getting my meal, I raised my meat, I was milking my cows. When I went to the store it didn't take a lot of money then to buy something. Nowadays they pay you good and when you go to the store they get you good. So I don't see no difference in it. I tell these young folks now, say, "Y'all holler for that higher wage. We worked from sun to sun, sometimes fifty cents a day." I said, "We're here." But these old folks raised their stuff at home with mules. It done got now where this younger race don't want to eat what you raise at home. They gonna live out the store.

I got to making syrup when I moved to Mr. Moye's place. He'd get his syrup every year from me. Told me, said, "Lucius, would you be interested in getting a mill? And put it over there at your place?" He said I could make the syrup and I could have all the toll I could make off it. He loved to see that mill going. Man, we used to make syrup. We had cane everywhere. Them boys of mine had got big enough to grind with that mill. We'd start at night after I knocked off, and we make syrup sometime till 11 o'clock that night. You see that kettle out there? It would hold a hundred gallons of juice.

There would be a heap of folks around. We'd fire up the kettle, and some of the boys would kill a couple of rabbits, bring 'em up there and wrap 'em and put that butter and stuff on 'em and roast 'em down in the ashes. We'd fire it up, gonna cook three runs of syrup. And we'd skim off that stuff that rises to the top, put it in the barrel. Call it buck. And some of the boys loved to drink that buck. Man, they'd get so drunk around that fire. That stuff'll make you drunk as whiskey. One night we were there, and Price Reese was there, and old John Powell and his wife Josie. Josie loved that cane, that buck. She kept going into that barrel, and she got so drunk. She was cutting up. Price, he was sitting there, he said, "Josie, you gonna fall in that fire. John, you better get her back away from here." John had the wagon, Price and her was in the car, and they carried her away from there. Price said when they got her home she didn't even know she was back down at the house. If you get drunk off of that stuff, you can't do nothing. You can't do a thing.

You can't have no fun with folks now. Now, I seen the time when Christmas time come, you could go to folks' houses serenading and all and have fun. But you go to a man's house now talking about having fun at Christmas time, you liable to get kilt. 'Course like they say, there's so much devilment going on these days, they don't know how to take it. Long back then, there wasn't that kind of stuff going on. I seen the time when around Christmas time a crowd would walk as far as from Lumpkin out here, and every house they'd get to, they'd stop. They'd go in there and everybody'd have fun; sometimes they'd eat cake, apples, oranges, things like that. All around the community, serenading. Folks would disfigure themselves, put dough faces on, put on wigs. Those dough faces — some of 'em are grey, some of 'em are red, and made up every whichaway;

had long beards and goatees and things on 'em. They would dress up that way and disfigure theirselves.

We went to a house one night, me and my children... my boy had done disfigured his face, and the other one had a big pillow across his stomach, had on a woman's dress. And me and my wife was there. Way I done, I went to the door and knocked on the door; all them was behind me. I went to the door — tap, tap, tap. The old man that lived there, he went to the door, he did, say, "Who is it?" I said, "It's nobody that'll hurt you." He opened the door, he did, and he was kinda behind the door. His wife was sitting over there in the corner and had a little baby, and when I walked in, he saw that crowd back there, he seen all them things, he laughed. We come right on in, and his wife was so scared she couldn't get up out of the chair. Lord, we did have fun there that night. Went on up to Ozelle's and got him, same way. That's the way folks used to have fun at Christmas. But you better not try it now. This day and time they're liable to kill you. The only thing they're thinking about is somebody coming there to break in and rob 'em.

And along back in them times, you'd be sick and the people in the community would visit you and help to see after you. But now if you get sick, ain't none of your friends gonna see after you. The first thing they gonna do is say, "Put him in the hospital." Say, "We ain't got time to fool around with him." But along then if a man or woman got sick, the house would be full of folks at night. I know my wife got sick, had epileptic spells or something, there was a house full of folks.

I was nine years old when I was baptized. Our

church was on the 27 Highway on the way to Cuthbert. They had a revival meeting on the first Saturday. Me and my brother both joined the church then, and we were baptized on the first Sunday. That was some cold water. We had a pool outside next to the church. They had it dug and boxed in. And a spring was just at the head where the water come into it. The water in that pool come out of that spring, come from under a big sweet gum under a bank. The water looked blue in there, and the sand in it was just as white as your hand. First Sunday in August, and that water was cold as ice. And that spring was where they got water for the church. And I toted many a bucket of water from there to the schoolhouse when I was a boy. There was a house there on that place, they got their water from there.

Early County, Georgia

The sermons and the songs in the churches just about the same now as they were then. Ours is run just like it was when I was coming up. Our pastor, he preaches here every first Sunday. That be our meeting day. On other Sundays, I can go to other churches. Yessir, I still go to church. I go to church and try to do what God put on me.

Well, we got so many preachers preaching now, but it ain't because God called 'em to preach. They preaching 'cause they done went to school and they practiced up to it. But when it comes down to that spiritual part, if a man don't know how to read and God calls him, he can preach just as good as that man who's got all them high faluting words. 'Cause even high faluting words don't mean nothing. The pure of heart, that means something.

Barber chair, weekend barber shop, Russell County, Alabama

Jessie Barnett's train, Henry County, Alabama

Meriwether County, Georgia

Barney Dickerson, Houston County, Alabama

Early County, Georgia

Clara Jewell, Randolph County, Georgia

CLARA JEWELL

Clara Jewell was born in 1912 in Henry County, Alabama. She has lived in the Lower Chattahoochee Valley all her life, and now resides in Cuthbert, Georgia. Her house is full of her fine needlework; a visitor cannot turn around without beholding some outstanding piece of crocheting, including tablecloths, doilies, and sugar-starched vases. Every bed in the house boasts one of the numerous beautiful quilts she has made over the years.

I been working in the field and cooking and house cleaning all my life; that's all I've ever done. I won't never forget trying to make my first biscuits. I was seven years old and I didn't know what to do. My mama was sick and she couldn't cook and I was the oldest. It was awful. I got the dough made up, but I didn't know how to knead that stuff and how to make biscuits out of it. Well, I started crying. Then Papa comes home and says, "Well, sugar, don't cry. I'll get 'em in there." So he just took a spoon and dipped 'em in the pan and put 'em in the stove. That's the last time I didn't know how to make a biscuit. If I had all I ever made since then, there wouldn't be room in this house to hold 'em.

My papa was a convict guard when I was little, then he was a foreman over the mule teams at a sawmill and later he became an overseer on this plantation. My mama and I worked the farm ourselves. We just had a one-horse crop. I can't remember how old I was when I started working on the farm, but I was real little, because anybody who could pick a boll of cotton would pick cotton.

There were seven of us kids in the family, one boy and six girls, and they raised nine orphans, so there were 16

of us children in all. The first four we took in were Mama's sister's. Her husband died and left her with the four boys. She was crippled with arthritis, rheumatism all over her body, couldn't even get up and get her a drink of water. The preacher went to see her one day and she was sitting there crying, said she didn't know what she was going to do, 'cause she couldn't handle the boys and they go off and leave her there and she wouldn't have no water in the house or nothing. So the preacher wrote my mama about the situation and I walked three or four mile to where Papa was and read him the letter. He got one of the trucks from the lumber company and went and got those boys that day after dinner. Then there was two Brannon boys, their father died and their mother married again and their stepdaddy was so mean to 'em till they just couldn't stay there. So they came and asked papa if they could stay with us. Well, Papa wouldn't turn nobody away. Then there was the three Polk boys that stayed with us for ages and ages.

We had to get a big house. We got a great big old antebellum thing in Columbia, Alabama. We had a round table that would seat 13 around it easy, and we could squeeze the little ones in between. It didn't bother us. We had plenty of milk and butter and eggs, and had our own meat and grease and growed our own vegetables, so we didn't never go hungry. But we had to work hard.

We had a rough time, no doubt about it, but then we had a good time. Mama was a wonderful musician, she could play anything that had music in it, it didn't matter to her what she picked up. We could entertain ourselves. We had a big old house and we had a lot of parties. People would come and we'd have sings. Mama played the organ and somebody else would play the guitar and somebody the mandolin. We had a good time. And my mama used to play guitar and fiddles at square dances around in the community. They used to play "Old Joe Clark", "Nigger in the Woodpile", "Red Wings" and stuff like that.

And, Lord, the good old revivals we used to have. Once a year there was a tent meeting. Everybody would quit working in the field early in the evening, go home and get dressed and go to that tent meeting. They would have the altar call and people would go down and get prayed for and testify as to how they'd been blessed during a meeting. And the singing was out of this world. Then, on Sunday, we'd take dinner and go spend the day. All the people in the area would come and we would just have a sing. It was great. It was somewhere to go. Back then, you know, there wasn't many places to go.

I pieced and quilted on my first quilt before I was 12 years old. I used to sit on Grandma's knees when she'd be piecing and I'd save all the little scraps and I'd cut little blocks out of paper and make little blocks out of the strings. I learned to crochet with strings we ravelled out of guana sacks, those sacks that fertilizer came in. "Red Fox", I remember that old red fox on there. You'd get the picture and writing on the sack out by bleaching it. We'd ravel out that string from the sacks and make a big old ball of twine and Mama taught me how to crochet with that twine. The first thing I ever crocheted with that twine was a bedspread, and it was the prettiest thing you ever seen. It was after I married that I learned to crochet by directions. I said, "Well shoot, somebody could write 'em; I surely ought to be able to learn to use 'em."

Mrs. Jewell made the tablecloth

Things are way different today than they use to be. Lord mercy, now I just go in the kitchen and turn on the faucet and get hot water to wash dishes. Turn on the water and there it is. Used to be you had to haul your water half a mile. And now I don't have to go out and get wood and build a fire. We didn't have gas heat you could turn on and light, and that was all there was to it. But, now, we just love our heater, 'cause see how nice and warm it is in here.

But the principles and the morals of the people back then was so much better than they are now. Just go to the beach and see all the disgrace. Some of 'em don't care whether they got on any clothes or not. If I dressed like that when I was coming up, they'd horsewhipped me. Might of beheaded me. I just don't know...people living together without being married, which is a disgrace. And you take most of the young people today, they can't be in your company five minutes without using a big long swear word. They got no table manners, most of 'em. So there's a big difference from the way I was brought up, and I still feel the same way today as I did then. And I'm glad I had the kind of raising I had and my daughter is raising her younguns that way, too.

JIMMY LEE HARRIS

Rarely does one have the pleasure of hearing a man as young as 45 sing and play old-time blues. Most bluesmen today are far older and past their primes. But Jimmy Lee Harris, who was born and still lives in Russell County, Alabama, is probably still as powerful and strong as he ever was, which is powerful and strong indeed.

My family were sharecroppers. When gathering time comes, you gather up the crop and sell it around Christmas. But when you gather it up, you don't get nothing. It was yours as long as you were raising it up, but when you got it together, it was the man's. You might owe him. You come out in debt, and you gotta go back in there next year just to try to break even, but you never break even. The only way you have to break even is to move. I've done seen people moving at night...that's the only way you had to go.

I started working in the fields when I was about eight or nine years old, working one day, school the next. When I was about 10 they finally dropped me out of school and put me in the field. I didn't feel too bad about having to drop out of school, 'cause I couldn't do nothing about it. But I knowed it was wrong, 'cause all the other children was going to school. It wasn't 'cause of me, it was 'cause of my parents and the man who own the place. We had a small family, about four of us in the family, that's all.

It felt all right out in the field 'cause there was nothing you could do about it. You had to be there. When you get to the end of the field, you go to the shade. When you get to the other end, you go to the shade. There weren't a tree in the field. But if the man around, you ain't gonna get in the shade.

My daddy made moonshine on the side, that was the only thing holding us up: moonshine. He was a sharecropper, too, during that time, because if you got caught making whiskey, the man gonna ask you where you work at, and you have to tell him where you work so the boss man can back you up. If you didn't have no job, you didn't have nobody to help you. The boss man say, "Well, he don't make no whiskey 'cause he work for me everyday." They say you better not make no more whiskey, then they drop the charge. Then you go right back and make some more.

We made it at night at a still hid out in the woods beside a ditch. Soon that morning before the sun come up, you get that fire and put that smoke out. I was about 11 years old, and I used to go down there and help my daddy make it. I got the wood and watched out for him. If anybody come in there, I hailed to him, and I gone and he gone.

I laughed one day, though. Let me tell you what I did. He gave me a shotgun and said, "You get up on that hill now, and if you see anybody, don't shoot them, just shoot up in the air and run." So when he started making whiskey, I went back up there, sitting on a stump, watching out, and I seen a squirrel. I forgot, you know, and that old squirrel was hopping around the tree, and I shot that squirrel, and my daddy took off. He thought I'd seen somebody, and I said, "Lord, I done messed up." Daddy run on home, and he was sitting there on the porch waiting for me to come home. I reckon he thought the police done got me. So

I come up the road with the squirrel in my hand, and he tore me up. Then we went back down there and fired it up and finished running it. Made about 33 gallons.

These days me and Eddie usually play at house-parties; you know, the folks who live in the house sell liquor and food to pay the rent. But they don't do it right any more. They want to fight...kill somebody. They start off good and end up bad, but back when I was a kid it was good. You could frolic all night long, till the break of day. Blowing harp, singing, patting, buck dancing, doing the yellow hammer and the black bottle.

The only instrument they had was the harmonica and sometimes the Jews harp. (Harris refers to the mouthbow as a Jews harp). But mostly it was just a harmonica. Neal Money would blow it; they called him the harp man. They didn't have no guitars. You couldn't hardly get a guitar back then, didn't have the money to buy one. Cheapest thing you could get was a harp, about 75 cents, or you could make a Jews harp or them old cane whistles. So Neal played the harp, and you could make music by your hands, clap your hands and sing while you're dancing. Songs like "Here-Rattle-Here" and "Call My Possum Dog, He Won't Come."

The first instrument I ever played was the mouth bow. I made one when I was nine years old. I would get me a good strong green stick, and put a piece of nylon string on it, get it real tight and put it to my mouth and pluck it. Me and Eddie used to put them to our mouths and try to make a sound like a guitar, 'cause we didn't have nothing to get no guitar with. But Mama and Daddy bought one when

Jimmy Lee Harris, Russell County, Alabama

I was about 12 years old, and we started playing that guitar then. The main person who taught us was a woman lived up the road named Seesa Vaughn. She taught me "16-20", "Don't the Moon Look Lonesome", "Rabbit on a Log", and "Sitting Here Looking a Thousand Miles Away."

I blow the harp without no harp. I make that sound like a harp with my mouth. I started doing that when I was doing some time on the chain gang in Raiford, Florida. I got three years in there for pulling a pistol on a man; I didn't shoot, I just drawed the pistol. But, anyway, I didn't have nothing to play in there, and I made that up in jail. I put my hands to my mouth and just did it, they all called me the Harp Boy. It sounded all right to the boys, so that's how we had our music.

Henry County, Alabama

Macon County, Alabama

Macon County, Alabama

Macon County, Alabama

EDDIE MARTIN

No one can ride by Eddie Martin's place in Marion County, Georgia, without noticing it. His living quarters and the constructions surrounding them are wildly flamboyant works of art. Almost everything inside his house — the furniture as well as the paintings and sculpture — are his creations. He even designs and makes his own apparel.

I was born July 4, 1908, 12:00 at night, in this county. My father was a sharecropper. I helped farm from the time I was big enough to hold a hoe handle — about five years old, but I picked cotton before that — about three years old.

I would draw whenever I had a pencil and a tablet, but it wasn't often I got them. I was always short of paper. And I had a father that didn't stand for no nonsense. He didn't wish you no better than he had hisself. He wouldn't allow my mother to read in the house. She had to go out in the privy in the back and set in the toilet to read novels and comfort magazines which ran serials. He always treated me as if he hated me with a passion. My mother had to show some kind of dislike for me as a child. There never was no affection, but I admired my mother. But I didn't admire my father, because he had nothing to be admired but hard work and toil and plowing a mule. I didn't like that myself, although I had to do it till I left away when I was 14.

I'd been working in the sawmills and I went down to get my pay and on the way back I caught the freight train. When I got off the freight train to go home, there was a passenger train there. I had about six dollars, so I decided I would go to Columbus. My brother in Columbus finally got me a job sweeping floors at a shop where he was foreman.

When I was 15, I decided to go to New York City. I wanted to get away, man. Even as a child I used to watch the Seminole train and I see them people sitting in the dining car with the silver and I used to say somebody sold me off of that train. I'd think, "Oh, if I could get big enough to leave here." Life around here wasn't the life for me. I wanted to be myself, and you couldn't be yourself around here in them days. I didn't feel Buena Vista was the place for me, because there was so much out there that I didn't know, that you couldn't know if you kept staying around here and becoming like the people that was around you. New York was where the action was — the music, dancing, drama. I wanted to go out where you could meet all kinds of people, and if I wanted to stay out all night long, it was my business and there wasn't nobody to ask me when I'm coming home or where I been.

So I drifted up there, and when I got to Jersey City, I had to stop and bum a nickel to get across on the ferry. I got to New York, and I just felt like it was wonderful. It was shining and pretty, and it was like a fairyland to me. The first thing I did, I went and stood on a corner. Hoping for a good, kind stranger. So one came along.

And there was this to that...this to that...then I got a room, and I lived. I'd go forth on the city every night. I put my hands in God's, man. I threw myself on the mercy of the world. At night when I would go forth I would pray to God, "I'm going forth tonight. What will it bring me tonight? My eyes is wide open… I seek and what comes to my arms I'll grab."

I met all kinds of people — actors, artists, writers, musicians, all kinds of people — models, prostitutes, pimps.

I stayed for 31 years, off and on. I used to come back and forth to home. I'd come back home and help my mother — my father had died — help my mother plow the farm up, break it up, lay it off to plant. Then I'd take off back to New York. Then I'd come back in the fall and help pick cotton, pull corn. See, when I got disgusted with the surroundings and the people I was mixed up with in New York, I was ready for a new scene. So I'd come here, as this was a haven for me; if I hadn't had this haven in time of storm, I don't think I would have made it. But whenever it would get too rough, I'd get across the river, head to the South and be here in a couple to three days, sometimes a day and a half.

I was living all through all of this and seeing so much of life and all the time I was meeting artists and I'd go to their studios and I would see what they did and sometimes they'd let me paint a little on a small piece of canvas and I could make some kind of movement there. And it rocked on and on and finally I thought, well, something's got to give here. So I read in Astrology Magazine from 28th of May, 1933, "You'll sit down and start to do something and you'll pursue that and follow that for the rest of your life." And I kept wondering, Oh my God, I'm going to meet someone that's got lots of money, and then I can get with the arts. But it didn't happen. I sat around and started drawing and things went on from there. And I had to paint and draw on pasteboard boxes, barrels, and sometimes I'd

just get to drawing on the walls in my apartment.

I began to get some money to buy canvas, paint, and brushes when I went into the psyche business in 1945. I began as a gypsy tea leaf reader — it wasn't gypsy really, Jews were in control of the tearooms — and then I started to read palms and then cards. It's a knack that you learn. I learned it in New York from just walking in the street; it was so much danger you had to learn to develop a third eye in the back of your head. You had to know what was going on behind you as well as in front of you. And that's how I started developing a psyche. You got to have instinct and you got to know them cards. Sometimes the cards will tell you everything, sometimes they won't tell you nothing. Then you got to penetrate that person's psyche barrier and get inside of them. I know how to turn on people, man, get into their inner sanctums, to their secret chambers, you know. I know how to hit to the bone.

I read cards for 12 years in New York. And then one day, I was sitting at the window, and a light came, like a big ball of fire, and it spoke to me and said, "Leave here, go home, go right now and pack your clothes and get your ticket and leave New York." So I went and cashed in my stubs and got my percentage and I went to the railroad station and bought a ticket, and I came back to my hotel and packed my stuff and arranged for all of my paintings to be shipped down here. And then I thought, oh my God, what a foolish thing you're doing, you're not doing bad here. I sat on my suitcase and I said, Should I really do this? And again that light came, and the voice spoke, says, "Go on and catch the train." So I caught the train and come on home. I figured if I could get hold of 25 or 35 dollars a week reading cards, I could paint with that.

The spirit spoke from that light, and I followed it. Because one time — around 1932 — I lay dead in there on that bed for three weeks. Not dead really, but my spirit left my body and went on a long spiritual journey. My sister told me that finally they was sitting in there at the fire one night and they said, "Well, we'll get word to Buena Vista in the morning to send a coffin, to get you buried." So that night I reached and came a great big figure, a man that had a long beard and hair straight up like the Watussis. And I came in front of this person, and he said to me, "You want to live and you want to return?" I says yes. He says, "You go back and you follow my way the rest of your life and you can survive. If you don't follow my way, you won't survive." So I have always listened to that voice, that inner voice, and seek counsel within myself about my decisions and about what I do.

I know that trying to do something creative and constructive is good. And there's a lot of things that I could teach and show people, but they won't accept me because I have no degree. Right away they say you're a shitass, you don't know nothing. They assume that attitude. I see some very fine artists that never went to school. School don't really have much to do with it, 'cause all they can teach you is the basics. It's up to you how you gonna grasp it, what you gonna do with it. You know, when you don't go with what's in style, you're an outcast. So I'm just an outcast on my own. Well, you know the wealthy people more or less control the art world. Columbus is so bound by social groups, but do they have anybody trying to develop any future poets, any future musicians, any future playwrights? They don't do a thing about developing nothing. Like everybody else in the United States, they all accept the curriculum coming out of New York.

Well, I don't care what people think about me. 'Cause nobody pays my rent, nobody don't put no bread in my mouth, except from my efforts. If you're gonna go through life worrying about what people gonna think about you, you're licked from the start. This society shuts out innovation. It's all right to innovate for the man with the big pile of gold but not to innovate for yourself.

I like to create my environment. That's why I like it back behind these walls, or right out there looking at 'em.

When I get out in that world — to get my groceries or whatever — I don't like it out there. I feel like this is my world, this is where I belong. I lived in the temples in the past. I've been a witch doctor, soothsayer, court jester, a king, a shaman. That's why I do these shaman chants sometimes; the shaman spirit will come to me. I don't prefer anyone's company, just me and God and my spirit. People may come in here to work or to see me, just sit here, later they go out. That's all I need people for. Of course, I realize that I'm growing old and if I get down I guess I'll have to have some-

body. But if I get down and can't produce something, I don't want to be here.

I take in customers only in the morning, so I can devote my afternoons to working with my guitar. I tape myself if I think I'm gonna do something worthwhile. See, I just sit down and get a rhythm going and take the words off the top of my head. I call it skimming — skimming over your memories. But it isn't so much what you say as how you say it, how you tone the words, how you work with your voice. When I was a kid, you see, I used to always hear these old darkies — there was always one or two around with guitars — and they'd be coming home Saturday night from this skin game, and they'd be singing them lonesome blues. So I always heard that, and it was always inspring. And I'd say, "Well, I'll learn how to sing someday."

Where did my style in my art come from? I used to always go see films of dances from India and Africa and all over the world, and those inspired my paintings. And I've always studied rhythm and motifs and people and I have always been concerned about nature and about being a real person. Real to yourself. And that's the hardest thing of all. To thine own self be faithful, Shakespeare said. The way I would interpret that would be: Go on and grasp life, and see it, embrace it, enjoy it, don't suppress yourself, don't live in a closet as most people do. They do it because of social mores. If you're too bold and brazen, they're quick to pass you on by. So be yourself. Gonna have to do a song on that one day.

Macon County, Alabama

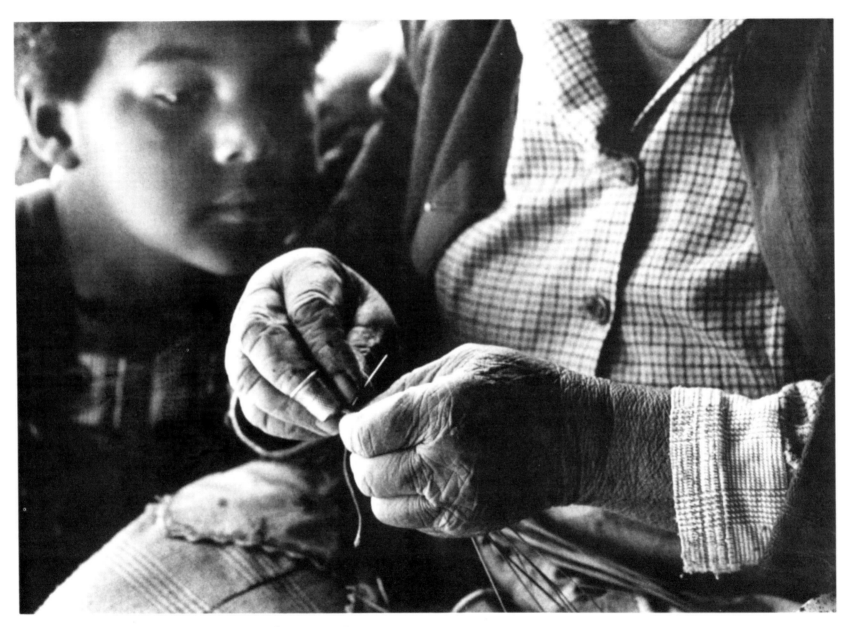

Watching the beginning of a pine straw basket, Talbot County, Georgia

Yard decoration, Early County, Georgia

Gene Jackson, Muscogee County, Georgia

Comer Grantham, Barbour County, Alabama

White Oak Basket: from start to finish, Tallapoosa County, Alabama

Sylvester Carlisle, Lee County, Alabama

SYLVESTER "PIG" CARLISLE

Sylvester "Pig" Carlisle is one of the very few tradi-tional blacksmiths in the Lower Chattahoochee Valley area. He still occasionally does small jobs in his shop in Opelika, Alabama.

When was I born? That's a big question. I couldn't tell you the date. I'm somewhere around 78 years old; at any rate, that's what they give me. Don't make too much difference, does it? I'm alive.

My daddy was a farmer. And, at the same time, he'd do the blacksmithing for the great big farms. They had seven or eight or nine families on these farms. My daddy do all the shoeing of mules, first one thing then another.

I started off farming when I got grown. We were farming on the halves. We didn't have nothing, the man had to furnish us everything. He was good about that. And he wanted his, and he wanted you to have yours. Like if you carry a bale of cotton down and sell it, he take half of it and I take half of it. And if it run a penny extra, know what he'd do? He'd say, "I'm gonna give you the penny this time and I'll get it next time." I couldn't differ with him. He wanted me to have mine, I couldn't complain about it. If he'd say, "Now that extra penny, I'm gonna take it," I could look at him about that a little. Well, we left from there. A man ain't suppose to eat up all that he makes in one year.

And George, my brother here, he come into town and went to work in a blacksmith shop down here. Then it wasn't long after that that I come in. Back in them days they had wagons — buggies I'm talking about — before there

were any trucks. We fixed the wheels on them, had steel tires. After a certain period of time they'd come to be shack-ly, and we'd tear the wheel down and rebuild it. And I made wheels. I made the axles out of a hickory tree that a man would cut down in the woods. Wasn't no car, no trucks to amount to nothing. But, boy, I built some nice truck bodies. I ain't saying it 'cause it's me. And we'd shoe mules, horses, fix plow stocks. Boy, I tell you the truth, I don't want to go back through those woods no more.

Why? I tell you the biggest thing — those damned old crazy-ass mules. Fooling with a crazy-assed mule that's never been shod. Old Man Jenkins come to the shop one day, said, "I got a good, big mule that ain't never been shod. I want you to shoe that mule so bad I don't know what to do." I told him to bring him to the shop. Mr. Dennis, my bossman, was gonna hold him and I was gonna shoe him. I walked up to that old mule and reached down to get his foot, touched him on the leg, he kicked the ground hard. Mr. Dennis got scared of him then. I got the rope and put it on him; I wasn't gonna let him hurt me. I commenced to working on his foot, he reared up. He had one foot tied and reared up with the other one and came back down. Mr. Dennis got the hammer and hit him up side of the head. Up he went again, and when he went up that time, he went up too far. He didn't come back down, he went over backwards, and when he hit the ground — that ground was hard — he hit the knob back there between his ears. They ain't never proved it. Killed him dead as a sardine.

I'll tell you something else about that, brother — a horse is worse than a mule. We had an old horse down there one day, and they had about three ropes on him and about three men right beside him holding him down on the ground. He commenced to raise his head, the help got scared and backed away, and he got up and down that road he went. We had that horse right down there beside the courthouse and he went down that road there at the side of the courthouse and when he got to running the ropes got to flapping and the more he'd run the faster he'd get. He ran from the courthouse to the depot — the 38 mail train was standing down there at the depot, and that horse ran down there and jammed up against that train. Ran into it just like it wasn't standing there.

I don't know how in the world I went through that and didn't get broke up or kilt. The Lord knew I was crazy. You take a old, gentle mule, he don't care what you do to him. But shoeing stubborn mules that ain't never been shod, that's the roughest side of blacksmithing. Get one in a tight, he won't listen to nobody. Ain't nobody ever fooled with their feets, see. And you go fingering around there, rubbing their legs — gonna pick up a foot — they're wondering what you up to.

Well, I quit working at the shop. I'll tell you, me and the bossman fell out. I was running a few minutes late — I had a old Model A Ford — I run up there in front and all of 'em were there working. I jumped out, got my work, and the bossman was standing there in the door, he just snatched that piece out of my hand. I just turned around, got in my car, and out I went.

I didn't mean to open up no shop here at home, but people commenced to running me down. I said I believe I'll build a little old shop, looks like folks gonna make me build one. Sometimes I think I could have done anything else and beat blacksmithing. My mind told me, Don't be a blacksmith, be something else. Me and my mind agreed, then I turned right back around and got into the mess. Ain't no blacksmithing to do now, ain't no mules to shoe...

Pig Carlisle's blacksmith shop

Henry Kirkland "gettin' out splits" for a white oak basket

HENRY KIRKLAND

Henry Kirkland of Henry County, Alabama, has been making white oak baskets for 63 years, and he is still making them. For visitors interested in his baskets, he enjoys jumping up and down on the cotton baskets to show just how well-made they are.

I was born in Henry County in 1906. I've lived in three counties, but not too far off. I was a farmer, I just never had no hankering to stray off from home. I always liked farming. Way back when I was coming up, that's about the only way we ever knew. It wasn't no factories in here. Now, a lot of people worked at sawmills. But that's heavy work. I was always too light for heavy work, and too heavy for light work. I rather be my own boss, as long as I could make a living. As long as you can satisfy your banker and your wife and children, you're a free man if you farm.

We plowed mules and we grew our own sweet potatoes, cane to make syrup, had a smoke house, killed enough hogs to make enough meat through a year almost. Used the lard, and we didn't have nothing much to buy in the way of groceries, just sugar, flour and coffee, rice, a few items like that. And had a garden the year round. We didn't have no telephone bills, light bills, drew water out of a well, and washed the clothes in a spring not too far from the house. Had a nice spring. We'd beat the clothes on a rock, and we'd run a trough made out of six-inch boards from the spring to the wash pots. We even made our own soap, potash soap, make it out of hog cracklins and potash and water, and when it got cold, you could cut it out in chunks like cheese. And,

boy, that stuff would get the dirt out of them overalls.

My daddy was a farmer. He died before I was 13 years old. He left seven children. And a widow. I've had the responsibility for a large family ever since I was 14 years old. We had 80 acres of old poor land, and I had one brother that was just 17 months younger than I am, me and him done most of the plowing and farming. I had to look out for what we had. There wasn't no welfare, you know, and I made baskets in the summer and sold 'em to keep groceries.

I started making baskets when I was 11. My daddy made 'em too, and my granddaddy and my uncle. I sold my first basket in 1917 for a dollar and a quarter. About two years ago, this farmer came by here wanting to buy a basket and I said they're thirty dollars. He said, "When I was a boy" — he's near 50 years old now — "my daddy used to buy 'em from you, I know how they last, they're worth it."

For the last five years, I've been going up five dollars a year on my baskets. Five years ago, I sold 'em for 15 dollars, now I'm getting 40 for the same kind of basket. But I'm still not getting no more out of it, 'cause when I go to the grocery store, why, they get it. I figure I don't get over two dollars an hour for my labor. Now, if I was able to farm like I used to and could grow peanuts and stuff like I used to, I couldn't afford to make baskets. I couldn't make a living out of it. But I'm drawing social security, and if I can grow me a garden and sell some baskets, I can live nice, and eat.

Chambers County, Alabama

Barbour County, Alabama

Talbot County, Georgia

Russell County, Alabama

Houston County, Alabama

Sumter County, Georgia

Russell County, Alabama

Mr. and Mrs. Oscar Skeen, Henry County, Alabama

OSCAR SKEEN

Nearly all of the older residents of Henry County, Alabama, know Oscar Skeen, because he provided music for so many years for them to dance by. In the early days, in fact, his fiddle was the only instrument heard at the numerous square dances in the area.

If I live to see the 22nd day of February, I'll be 88 years old. I've lived in Henry County all my life except for one year. Stayed in one place all the time, ain't nothing in moving about. I've lived a Christian life, honest man all my life, don't take nothing that don't belong to me, and that's the reason I've lived as happy a life as I've lived.

I wan't but four or five years old when I started working in the field. Had to. Toting fertilizer, dropping corn, dropping peanuts — by hand, you know — behind my daddy. Brought up poor. All we had to wear was overalls. Didn't have no shoes to wear. I remember the first pair of shoes my daddy bought me. I was seven years old. They was old brogans, you know, with a brass cap on the toe of 'em.

We couldn't get no money to live on hardly, it was a awful time. But there's some more ahead of us, worse than them was. Lord, I hate to say it, but I don't know how the old people like us are gonna make it. We don't get nothing but a little old social security check, and we can't live on it no more from one month to the next.

The earliest memory I have was when my daddy went to Columbia and bought him a mule, the prettiest mule I ever saw in my life. I was a little ole boy, wasn't but four or five. And that mule was so gentle, he just licked us and I run under its smooth belly. Like to scared my mama to death. She said don't you get under that mule's belly. It was a red mule, red all over, sort of white-looking under her neck. She just loved us children, she'd smell of us, you know. Five years old, young mule, my daddy raised our family with it.

I bought my first fiddle when I was seven years old. My daddy gave me and my brother a cotton patch, and we made a bale of cotton on it. My brother bought him a suit of clothes and I bought me a fiddle. Give eight dollars for it. And I've had one ever since. I could already play one when I bought it. Just by going about to square dances in the country at night, and get down beside the fiddler and just watch his movements in his hands. And get the tune in my mind.

I was 19 years old when I got married and my wife was 16. Sixty-eight years we've been married, me and that woman there. We growed up together, we had known each other since we were babies. When we was coming up we walked to school together. I got drunk just one time in my life, about two or three months before we got married. Fellow give me some whiskey, wanted to make me drunk to where I'd quit going with her. And, by golly, I just smelled the bottle and I stayed drunk for two days and nights, didn't know nothing, just crazy. And I never have drank another drop since. I've certainly been blessed, we've both been blessed. We loved one another back then and still do, and I intend to be her husband, a true husband to her, as long as I live. We just been good to one another. I was a fiddler and I never went off without her. She went with me and beat the straw.

We went to playing for square dances, just me and her. I played the fiddle, she'd beat the straw for the rhythm. Lord have mercy, if it wasn't pretty, you've never heard nothing. As pretty as could be. Usually about 15 couples, neighbors you know, would come to dance. And they pay me and her so much a set. Each couple would pay a dime a set, and we wouldn't never make less than a dollar.

I won first prize at every fiddler's convention I ever went to. I played at courthouses in five counties in Alabama and Georgia, and I won the first prize at every one of them.

At the courthouse in Blakely I won every prize they give, five of 'em. They give every one of 'em to me. I told 'em, "I think you made a mistake, some of 'em was good enough to win some of 'em." He said, "We give it to the man that won it." I said, "Well, thank you."

I just loved fiddling, always loved it, and I can't hardly stand to hear one played now, I just want to do it so bad myself. My fingers has got stiff, you know, and I can't play like I used to, the movement like I had. But I still love it, will love it as long as I live.

Talbot County, Georgia

Barbour County, Alabama

Chambers County, Alabama

Stewart County, Georgia

William Grant making a washboard, Russell County, Alabama

Herman Wadsworth, Talbot County, Georgia

HERMAN WADSWORTH

Born near Tuskegee, Alabama, Herman Wadsworth begin painting at an early age. At the age of 76, he goes often to the shed in the back of his house that serves as his studio and paints landscapes and portraits. His mailbox lies on the county lines of Talbot and Taylor.

I've been on my own ever since I was 14 years old. My mother married a second time; when she did that, I took off. Couldn't get along with my stepdaddy, tell you the truth. He was always telling me I ought to get out and get me a job, go to work, he couldn't afford to feed me, all that kind of talk. That kind of cuts...makes you feel like you're not wanted, you know.

I just didn't want to cause any disturbance between my mother and him, so I packed me a bag, went to Columbus, Georgia. But I had to lie about my age to get a job, because they wouldn't hire you at that age. I told 'em I was 16; that's the only way I could get a job. I had 10 or 15 dollars, something like that, when I left. I didn't have much. Wasn't no way to get ahold of no money those days. It was nip and tuck, brother.

I rode a little old train to Columbus. They had a little old train come in at Tallassee, you know...tell you the truth, I hoboed. I caught a freight. I caught a freight when I left Columbus, too. I rode freights quite a bit when I was a kid. Get from place to place, you know. I traveled, I went to Florida and Chicago, followed the job, just here and yonder, catching freights.

I remember one night...I had a buddy I run around with, and we both had bought us new pairs of white overalls — we were painters and paper-hangers — and we were waiting at the shed down there in Birmingham for that Pan American to come in there. We were gonna ride the blinds to Decatur, Alabama. We crawled up between them blinds, and a special agent climbed up on the other side. He had a gun pointed at me, longest barrel pistol I ever saw. He said, "Now, boys, you can't ride this train, this is a mail train, you're gonna have to get off." I looked at that gun; I thought, we'll get off. Yeah, we got off. So we went out to a freight yard out in north Birmingham and caught a freight out of there.

One time, another buddy and I caught a freight coming out of Chattanooga, Tennessee, was gonna ride it to Huntsville. We got in a box car, open box car, coming down Lookout Mountain, a lot of curves and all. And somebody up in the engine, he'd wave at us, motion you know, and we'd wave back like kids will do. He was trying to get us back inside where nobody wouldn't see us, but we didn't have sense enough to realize it. Finally we stopped at an old place called Clarksville just above Huntsville, stopped at the water tank there, and they come down and made us get off. Told us, "We tried to get you boys to get inside and you wouldn't do it. Somebody saw you now, done give us orders to put you off." They put us off there and we caught a passenger train, rode the blinds, come on into Huntsville. It stopped at the water tank in Huntsville, so we got off on the blind side.

Back in those days around there, see, if they caught you hoboing or if you didn't have the price of a meal in your pocket, they'd put you on the gang for 30 days. Had to dig a

ditch they had up there, about two or three miles long and 50 feet wide and 30 feet deep, by hand shovels and picks. Hoboes, guys passing through the town without the price of a meal in their pocket, they called 'em vagrants and put 'em on the gang for 30 days.

I did all kinds of work. Painting houses, working in mills and in foundries, construction work, anything I could get to do. Like I told my wife when I married her, "I'm gonna make you a living if I have to get down there and dig a ditch." And I've had to do that a time or two, but I fed my family.

I sold the first picture I ever painted for a dollar and a half. It had a winding trail from the bottom of the picture on up to the top and I had three different trees painted on the side of this trail. And this lady who run this dry goods store there in Huntsville, she saw it, she said I want that picture. Said, "What'll you take for it?" I told her. She says, "I want you to write on there 'As I live I grow'." See, the first tree on the trail was a small tree and the next one was a little larger and then there was a big tree. She wanted to use that slogan for her business. She put it in her show window and gave me a dollar and a half.

I've painted pictures of nearly every town I've ever worked in. And when I was stationed in the Marshall Islands, I used to paint big pictures of the sailors' girlfriends from little photographs they had. I'd tell them my price, and I'd say, "If you're not satisfied with it, you bring your buddies along with you, and if they don't like it, you don't have to buy it." I used to paint a lot of pictures on the coconuts they had over there. Paint a ocean scene on there, maybe a coconut tree or two, a sunset. I painted gobs of those; ain't no telling how many I painted. The guys would want to send them home to their families as souvenirs. See, I had a lot of spare time, and I was the type that didn't sit around and grieve myself. I liked to keep my mind occupied, keep busy with something. I'd seen too many guys just crack up... Tell you the truth, all the guys wasn't killed just in battle. A lot of 'em killed theirselves. I even cut hair in the service. They set me up a tent and they told me, you're the base barber. Cut hair after my regular hours; shoot, I'd do anything just to pass the time.

When I've finished a painting I really like, I feel better when I show it to several different ones and they tell me they think it looks nice. It don't make me mad when they tell me they don't like it. I've learned to take that. But it's encouraging when you do something and you think maybe someone else likes it as well as I do myself or maybe better. It kinda helps you a little bit.

I have been married 30 years, lived here ever since '46. When I bought this place, it was all growed up in bushes, there wasn't a pine tree in sight, wasn't a tree in this yard. Every tree you see in this yard I set out myself. That tree over there, I dug it up when it was about two foot high and set it out. That walnut tree, I dug it up in the ditch over yonder when it wasn't but a foot high; all these cedar trees, I set 'em out. You see those pecan trees — I set those out, my little girl used to jump over 'em. She's about 26 years old now.

Ophelia Wilson, Barbour County, Alabama

OPHELIA WILSON

Ophelia Wilson was born 59 years ago in Barbour County, Alabama, which she has never left. She has bottomed chairs with corn shucks since she was a young girl.

My father got both his hands cut off when I was four or five years old. He got 'em cut off in a steam sugar cane mill. He was feeding the mill and his hand got caught in it. He said he threw his other hand in it to save his body. See, it had so much power, it would have got his head and all. But after he got his hands cut off, he kept on working in the fields, just like everybody else. He worked with a scoop instead of a hoe. He would hold it between his arms and he would take his foot and push it down in there and scoop it lightly. And he would get all them little pieces of grass by pulling 'em up with his toes.

I remember the first day my mama carried me to the field, trying to learn me how to chop cotton. She told me how to thin out the cotton plants. The cotton would be so full, there would be too many in one hill, so we'd chop it out. "You thin it out and you leave two stalks in a hill and over here you leave two more..." Finally she let me do it, she would get on the row with me til I learned how. Then I would take the row. Go on and do it myself.

Oh yeah, I used to be a good cotton picker. I have picked five hundred pounds of cotton — two and a half in the morning, two and a half in the evening. You can ask anybody around here. Picking cotton all day long felt good to me... Back hurt, little bit, but it didn't bother mine bad. I'd just get down there and crawl. I'd put on these here knee pads to keep my knees from getting sore. Put those things on, just crawl and drag your sack on your shoulder. I enjoyed picking cotton because if you didn't you'd just get discouraged. Now I had a sister, she didn't like it — everytime she got in the field she'd have a headache. After dinner, often we came back to the field, she'd be standing there just crying and don't want to work, she would be sick. Now, see, if I had been like that...

Me and one of my sisters used to pick up peanuts that was left on the ground after we got through working the crop. We would sell 'em. One time me and her picked up over a ton of peanuts off the ground. And they say, "What you gonna do with them?" I said I was gonna get me a gold tooth. Some of my other brothers and sisters already had one. That's what I wanted, a gold tooth. Wasn't nothing wrong with my tooth, no, I just wanted one of solid gold over it. That's what I got. And everytime I had my picture taken I'd just sit there and smile big and it'd be shining.

To wash our clothes we had to go down to the springs, carry our clothes down the hill to the spring 'cause we didn't have no water up on the hill, no well or nothing. A spring come out from under the hill, and we would take the tubs and things down there. And then bring 'em back up and hang 'em out. And if we had a spot in any of them clothes, we had to take 'em down and go right back down there and wash 'em again. And then after the clothes would dry, we had to pick up sticks to burn and make a fire. We had these smoothing irons, don't know nothing 'bout no electric. We'd make a fire, and then set the iron down in there, and it get red. And you just iron. Lord, I don't know

how in the world we made it. I say to my children, "Y'all have a good time."

Most of the sickness back then they would use home remedies. When they have a cold or something like that, they would go out and get these little duck bills and some of that green pine tar and a little rabbit tobacco, and they would take that and put it in an old black kettle and make tea. For chicken pox they used to give you shuck tea, you know, from corn shucks. And then they would take the child to the chicken house and hold his head down and let the chicken fly over his head.

When a boy came calling he had to leave at ten o'clock. The peoples had these old straw brooms, that's what they would use to let you know the boy had to go. About 9:30, you could hear Daddy and Mama walking around in the house; they be just walking, and looking and peeking, I reckon. So at 10 o'clock if the boy ain't gone, they take the old straw broom, throw it down, it's time to go. Throw the broom into the room where you be sitting with your boyfriend.

I met my husband — he's dead now — when he was in the service. When I got married I thought I was getting rid of doing all this hard farmwork, I thought it would kinda make my life easier. My husband said when he got out of the service, "We gonna get you a brick house, I want to make you happy." After he got out of service they built me a house. They got some logs and made these rough boards and made us a house. Had about three rooms. And I said now I was doing good and I'd be happy. I was happy for a while, but I wasn't happy living in a... I wanted to live in

Barbour County, Alabama

a brick house or something like that.

I do housework for people sometimes now. That and making chair bottoms is what I do to make some money to add to my VA check. I just do housework to try to pay my bills up. They don't pay you much for housework. Yesterday I worked from 7:00 to 3:30, they give me 12 dollars. I just let them pay me what they can. I just work and then they give me something for it.

Ooo, Lord, I don't know how many chairs I've made. I've made some for the white and some for the col-ored. There's no telling how many I've made. I used to bottom four and five chairs in a week. I don't get but three dollars a chair. People don't understand how much work it takes to get those shucks and make a chair bottom out of 'em. They don't want to give me no more money than that. So I just about stopped making 'em. It takes me a day and a night to bottom a chair and I can make ten dollars a day doing housework somewhere. If I could make that on a chair, I wouldn't go to work. I'd just sit here and bottom a chair. 'Cause I love the job.

Early County, Georgia

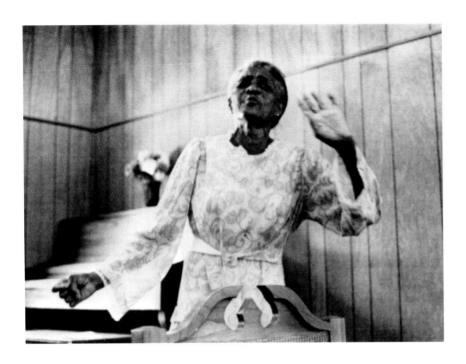

Macon County, Alabama

Mrs. Albert Johnson, Russell County, Alabama

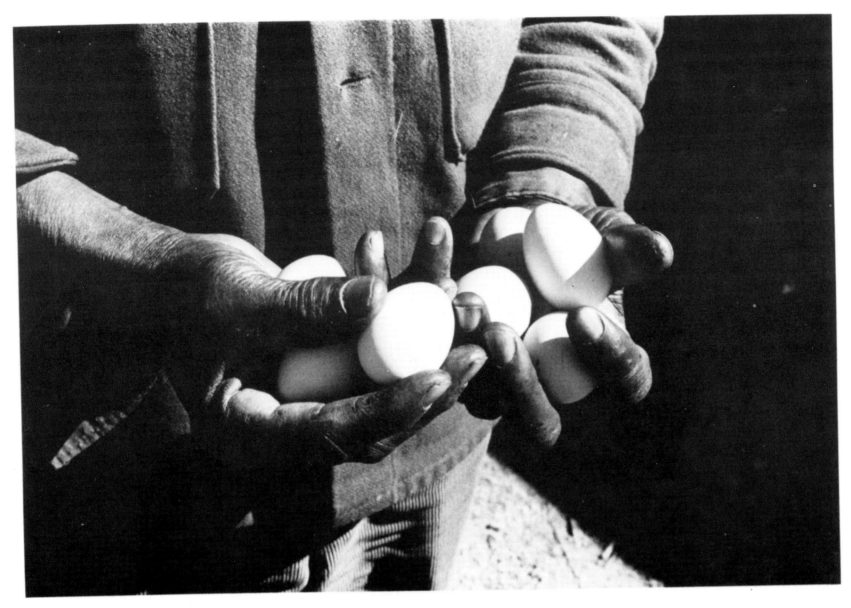

Stewart County, Georgia

Doug Booth, Houston County, Alabama

B. T. Foote, Macon County, Alabama

B. T. FOOTE

Beatrice Foote, whom everybody calls B. T., was born in 1908 in Macon County, Alabama, where he still lives. He supplemented his income from farming by playing guitar at county dances, and was an important influence on other blues singers in the area.

My Mama died when I was three weeks old. So my daddy gave me and my sister to our granddaddy and grandmama, and so they raised us. My mama died of a thing they called child bed fever. My grandmama, she the one that grannied me. You know, she was a midwife, a herb doctor, she made medicine for my mama but she never could get her started back.

Those old midwives would go get roots out of the woods and make medicine. Lot of old stuff in the woods such as black snake root, sasparilla, dollar leaf, prickly ash root, black haw root, butterfly root, queen delight, bull nettle. Those midwives, they knew some things from their experience. Mama — that's what I called my grandmama — she was kind of like a doctor. Now she learned all that herself, 'cause you can't go to school for it. Everything was handed down to you.

When I was a child, she would take me around with her in the woods during the summer when this stuff was green and growing. She would put a stick in the ground by a plant and tell me, "Buddy, remember this. This is sasparilla root." And carry me somewhere else and stick another stick by a different plant. She put those sticks there so we would know where the roots were in the fall of the year when the plants died out. She taught me all the different kinds of roots she made medicine with. So when a lady with the body trouble would come see her at night, she would send me to the woods to get the right kind of root. She wouldn't go out at night, you know, but she didn't care about me getting out in the dark. She would say, "Buddy, go get me a piece of butterfly root," or "Bring me a piece of black snake root." So I just go on over the hill and find the stick we put in there by the kind of root she want, dig down to that root, cut off a piece of it, cover the hole back up, and stick that stick back in there. Go on to the house with it, she'd wash it good and make the sick lady tea and give it to her and say, "Well, now, you go home and you take this by my direction." She knew what she was doing.

I remember one time when a disease broke out that they called some kind of flu. Practically everybody took that flu. And my grandmama hadn't lost a patient. So this white doctor over at the hill had lost three of his cases from that flu and he came over to my grandmama's house in a buggy, and he said, "Annie, what you using that you haven't lost a patient?" She told him that she was using whiskey in her medicine. And she told him all about the roots and herbs she was using. But he said, "I don't know that kind of stuff, about that stuff in the woods." Well, my grandmama said, "Well, you just practice using a little whiskey in your medicine, and you'll see how much better it will be." A little whiskey. But it would have to be good, pure, coal-made whiskey. And she told him how to dose it and how many times a day to dose it with that particular flu. So he began to use the whiskey with his medicine. And he didn't lose nary another case. They all got well.

All of that is cut out now. No more midwives. My grandmama knew what she was doing, and she would make that medicine, and it were doing them peoples good back there. But, yet, they didn't know when a fever was high or when your blood was too low or too high or nothing like that. They didn't know whether the lady with child was eating the proper foods. So all that was cut out on account of so many babies being born with afflictions. So now everything goes to the hospital.

Now, we still got a couple of them tooth-headed doctors. These root workers and fortune tellers. Both of 'em I know are ladies. I carry a lot of people to see 'em. See, they come from other counties hunting the place and some tell 'em, "See Foote, Foote can tell you." And they come here and I carry 'em to see the doctor. I don't know what their trouble is, but they say they getting good benefit behind it.

One time I took my son to see one. He had come to have funny little fits, acting funny, you know, peculiar. Well, my daughter beat up a boy pretty bad — she was older — and the boy goes home and tells his daddy. Well, not long after that, we was going to pick cotton at this farm and we was walking through the woods, and we come to a sand bed — pretty, white sand bed. Somebody had smoothed that sand bed off pretty with their hand, so me and my wife walked around it looking at it, wasn't thinking about the little boy, and he just walked right through it.

Well, not long after that, he come to acting funny, and sometimes he would start hollering and crying with his stomach hurting. We took him to the doctor. The doctor thought he was wormy, he give him medicine, but none of it did no good. Eventually, the doctor said. "Well, Foote, I don't see nothing wrong. He's not wormy, his blood is all right, his heart is all right, I'd advise you to go to a tooth-headed doctor, like you were talking about."

So we carried him to this lady, and she got out her crystal ball and set it on the stove to warm. Then she set it on the table and told us what she saw. She told about my girl beating up this boy and said that boy's daddy did this. She told about that sand bed, how pretty it was swept out and how that boy's daddy had put some mess in that sand bed, and that was what made my boy sick. She said this boy's daddy carried the boy to Montgomery to a root-worker and got this mess, and he put it in the sand in the path that he knew we walked along everyday to go to the fields. She said he was actually after my girl that had whipped the boy, but she didn't walk in it. Well, that lady could see that just as clear, and she didn't know nothing about what had happened, and she described that boy that my girl beat up and her daddy and mama to a T. And she gave my wife some sort of medicine to give my son, and he got well.

See, a lot of them root workers work both ways. They'll give you some mess to make somebody sick or make 'em have bad luck, and they'll take that stuff, that spell, off of you too. 'Course Lonnie Wright, he was a man root worker that's dead now, he said he didn't do nothing to hurt nobody, he helped people. If anybody did something to you, he'd break it up. 'Course some root workers will turn it back on the other person.

It are true, really are true, peoples can do that. I remember when I was a real young man, wasn't thinking about marriage, running everywhere, I was going to see this pretty young gal. Me and another fellow that played guitar would go see her and her sister. Well, I couldn't get up nothing for her. I would play the guitar and my friend and his gal would dance and then they would go in the back room and have some fun. And he'd come back and start to playing, now I'm dancing with my gal, and as long as I'm dancing with her it's out front like a pole. And she'd tell me, "Come on, maybe we can do something now." Minute she layed down, I climb up there and touch her, down it'd go. And everytime I'd be with her, that's the way it would go.

So one day I was walking by this man's house — he was Old Man Spencer Pace — I didn't know nothing about the man. He stopped me and looked me hard in the face and says, "Stay here till I come back." He went in the house and come back with a wash pan and a rag and little bar of soap. He said, "Come here, pull up your sleeve, wash your hands clean with that soap." So I did. Then he said, "Come on up here to me." I walked up there to him. He told me to ball my hand up in a fist just as tight as I can. So I balled it up, and he said "All right, open it right here in front of my face." I did that, he looked at me, said, "Listen, I'm gonna tell you something. From your house going west, there's a lady over there you like and she likes you. You can't have no luck with here. Now, you think it's your fault, but it's not in you. It's that other fellow who she put down. He done cut off her lead, because he can't get there. He figured if he couldn't go there and couldn't have no fun with her, he gonna fix it where nobody else can. So somebody worked up this trick for him."

He told me he knew I didn't believe in the stuff he could do, which I didn't; I didn't have no faith. He said he was gonna show me it were true. He said, "I'm gonna fix it where you can have some luck with this gal." He went in the house and come back with some hot grease in a rag. Said, "Whenever you get ready to go over to her house, the first branch you get to, you straddle that branch, let all your clothes down from the waist, then grease yourself good with this stuff, and reach down and get your hands full of water, and splash it around your navel. Do that three times. Then say these three words what I'm giving you to say. Put on your clothes, go on where you're going and you'll find out this here gonna work. Maybe then you will have a little confidence in what people can do, 'cause things can be done." And that treatment worked.

I played guitar for every frolic in this area. Then I went to playing for white folks' dances. I'd play at these set dances. At the colored dances each couple paid 25 cents a set, and the caller would get 10 cents and I'd get 15 cents. The people that had the house where the frolic was at would sell whiskey and food. At white folks' dances, they didn't sell nothing. The boy would pay 25 cents for him and 25 cents for his girl, and when the dance was over, the house man would split the money with me.

At the colored dances, I'd play spirited instrumental pieces. Just music to dance by. I be frailing it, feel natural, you know. And the caller would stand by me and he'd be

calling out, and they was moving by his call. They would do these breakdown dances, and they had a dance they called the Sixteen Handed Reel. Now, white people, they didn't dance like we danced. They liked to waltz, you know; they like to just slide, kind of two-step. They didn't do like colored people — boom-a-loo, boom-a-loo, boom-a-loo — jumping up and all like that. They slow dragged, "Come Home, Little Willie, Come Home", and all like that. And sometimes they danced fast, skipping all around . . . pip-tiddy, pip-tiddy, pip-tiddy.

It was always somebody at a dance that's come there for no good. So I was playing one night for a white people's dance. And there's an old white man with a black hat, wide brim, he sitting in the corner, had a mouthful of tobacco, old tobacco spit coming down all over his whiskers. I was playing, and they were dancing beautiful. So eventually this old white man came and stood by me. I just kept playing. Well, in a while he touch me; I looked at him. He said, "What you looking at?" I said, "Nothing." I was looking at the girls dancing, you know, they dancing so pretty. He said, "By God, play your music and look at your damn guitar." I said, "You mean I got to play with my eyes shut?" Well, then, another man came out with a old switchblade knife, the handle candy striped, and he opened the blade and started moving it stabbing fashion. He said, "By God, play your music and shut your damn mouth. You done said enough, goddammit, to be running." I didn't shut my eyes, but just ducked my head and played. And the man stood right there by me with the knife, and every now and then he'd snort just like a horse. Til the dance was over with.

So I made up my mind then that I'd just better quit this thing. And the other thing that made me stop was they was beginning to get these little old record players, with a stack of records, to dance by. Somebody would stand by that thing, and when one record played out they'd put another on. And they danced by that. And then at these here beer joints, they had these piccolos, put a nickel in, play a record, and they dance by that. So they just got to the place where they wasn't messing with a guitar picker. A man with a guitar couldn't make no money.

'Course, I kept singing and playing them old corn songs. I made 'em up, put some music to 'em, called 'em blues. I'd get a song perfect, at home by myself, and then I go somewhere and play it, and the people just be took off their foots; they ain't heard that before.

I could play a great number of church songs too, and old people would get me to come to their house to play church songs, and they'd sing. And somebody come through there, they'd think somebody having church. A lot of old people would get happy; the spirit would come to them, and they would get happy, and start crying and shouting. And sometimes I would do the playing and singing, like "Motherless Children Have a Hard Time." I just couldn't play that in places where somebody did have a mother that died when they was young. They'd get to thinking about how they come up without a mother, and how hard it was . . .

See, the idea of it is a mother comes to be practically all you got. A daddy all right in his place, but he's not like a mother. My mama was dead, but my grandmama was a mother in the place of her. A plenty night I would be disturbed, sometime my arm would be out from under the quilt, and my grandmama would pull my arm back in, and cover me up. Protecting me, keeping me warm. So you look at it like that, and that makes a mother have a great responsibility and a lot of care for her child. So a child should be very careful how he treat his mother. And then you read in the Bible where it say, Honor Thy Mother and Father. A person supposed to honor his mother, and not only his mother, but all people old enough to be your mother.

It done changed now, because children are not raised like that no more. You see, when a baby born now, he don't even know whether he got a breast or not; they buys the bottle and the milk and stuff before the baby born. And the nipples. They don't never see a mother's breast. It used to be a child born, he would get to nurse his mother. He got the full nature of his mother. So now they go to feeding him off some other kind of milk — all kind of cow milk — well, he just don't have the mother nature. Then when he grow up he get to the place where you can't do nothing with him.

And, nowadays, they can go to these supermarkets and these Seven-Elevens and buy all these Playboy magazines. These stores have all them kind of books hanging up there. Women books, men books. The children go buy it, you see. It presses that knowledge in their head too fast. It supposed to come in there as he grows, gradually, and not forced in there. He gonna learn these things, but let age bring it. But if you force it in there, a lot of times it takes him off his foots, and you can't do nothing with him. You teaching him one thing and somebody else teaching him something else.

You'll find that people nowadays don't have that good old spirit. Peoples years ago all doing the same thing. And that was farming. And one child couldn't look over the other one. And in that, look like people was more happier. People would get out in the fields picking cotton, they didn't put theirself on the strain, they just went out there and went to work . . . laughed . . . talked . . . and some of 'em would start singing, and first thing you know all them folks in the field singing, especially the women. Sometimes, I'd get out there and get to plowing that old mule, and he walking right, strike me a good old hymn, just singing and plowing. When 12 o'clock come, I ain't thinking about tired, just done sung that away.

Russell County, Alabama

Russell County, Alabama

Houston County, Alabama

Lee County, Alabama

NOTES ON THE ATTACHED CD SET

The Lower Chattahoochee River Valley creates a border between the states of Georgia and Alabama for a distance of over one hundred and fifty miles. This land, abundant in natural resources, was opened for settlement in the early nineteenth century. In the sixteen decades since, people of cultures from around the world have, by choice or circumstance, settled in this region. These people have blended the traditions which they brought with them from their homelands into a society rich in its variety of customs and folkways. Diverse in religion, skills, speech and attitudes, these people have blended the traditions which they brought with them from their homelands into a society rich in its variety of customs and folkways.

Diverse in religion, skills, speech and attitudes, these people have provided us, the present generation, with a bountiful legacy of traditions in music, art and workways. It is this rich legacy, a gift to us from generations past, which we now proudly celebrate in this anthology of music traditional to the Chattahoochee Valley.

FRED C. FUSSELL
Project Director

This album contains a large variety of traditional and old-time music recorded in the Lower Chattahoochee River Valley area in 1980 and 1981. All the musicians featured on the records are traditional in the sense that none of them received formal instruction and in most cases learned their skills from music makers in their families. When asked who taught them, almost all the musicians said they "picked it up" on their own, meaning that as children they watched the movements and listened to the sounds made by musicians they knew and then tried their own hands on the instruments. There are three major sources for the particular songs on this record album. Many of them have been handed down from generation to generation, the identity of the composers being unknown.

Folk music of all types has been available on phonograph records for almost 60 years, and some of the songs here are adaptations of commercial recordings. Others are original creations of the artists featured on the album.

When "old-time" music was not old-time — that is, when it was the popular music of the day for many people in the Chattahoochee Valley — it was usually played at social gatherings. Sacred music, of course, was sung and played in the churches. White secular musicians usually performed at "stage shows" in schoolhouses and on the numerous live local radio programs in the area, in addition to playing for square dances at people's homes and beer taverns. Black secular musicians usually played at "country frolics," at Saturday night fish fries and at barbecues where members of the community would gather for round dances. These events are near extinction today, and the musicians who still play traditional music usually do so at small get-togethers or by themselves for their own satisfaction. Only a few of the musicians on this album made a living as performers, although most supplemented their incomes by their music.

Born in 1926 in Montgomery, Alabama, **DOUG BOOTH** began playing a small four-string banjo at the age of 12 and immediately moved to the guitar. After getting out of the Navy at the age of 20, he began playing hillbilly music professionally, either solo or with groups. He was constantly on the road, playing guitar, mandolin, fiddle, or bass at beer taverns and over the radio. He retired from the music field a number of years ago and now lives in Dothan, Alabama. Booth and **JOE BERRY**, also of Dothan, get together to jam on weekends and occasionally perform at local functions.

PRECIOUS BRYANT was born into the very musical Bussey family in 1942 in Talbot County, Georgia, where she still resides. Her father played the guitar, banjo, fiddle, and a cane fife. She mastered her first instrument, the ukulele, when she was five years old and started picking guitar when "it was bigger than I was." She is adept at blues, church songs, and dance pieces.

CLIFF DAVIS was born 68 years ago in Alabama, moving to Stewart County, Georgia, his present home, as a small child. A farmer, he used to sing field hollers to relieve the tedium of his work.

THE DICKERSON FAMILY of Houston County, Alabama, is a musical family indeed. "It used to be said," stated banjo picker Alfred Dickerson, "that if a Dickerson hadn't learned to play an instrument by the time he was 12, he would be knocked in the head." Alfred Dickerson's father, most of his uncles, great uncles, and cousins, and seven of his brothers, including fiddler Barney Dickerson, played some stringed instrument in the old-time hillbilly style. The surviving members of the family who are still musically active get together every Christmas for a musical celebration .

RAY FAVORS was born in Manchester, Georgia, in 1941 and moved to LaGrange, Georgia, in 1958. Having learned to hambone, buck dance, and tap dance at Saturday night fish fries, he picked up spare change as a child dancing on the streets of Manchester for tips. He started beating a small washtub to provide rhythm for a guitarist friend, and since has "beat the bottom out of three tin tubs." **JAMES LLOYD** is in his middle seventies and has lived in LaGrange most of his life.

WILLIAM GRANT, 73, was born near Pittsview, Alabama, where he still lives. He was given a harmonica (harp) one Christmas, and he says he learned to play it while sitting on a plow in the fields. "I played at parties in the countries," he said. "I used to pick guitar, but I come to religion and I put the guitar down. I promised the Lord I wouldn't fool with a guitar no more, but I didn't promise Him I wouldn't fool with a harp. I always keep a harp."

Born in Barbour County, Alabama, in 1924, **COMER GRANTHAM** started playing the fiddle at the age of six His father, whom Grantham remembers as a "good corn fiddler," played fiddle ,at square dances while his mother "beat the straws" against the fiddle strings to provide rhythm. Grantham remembers the days when every small town in the area had an annual fiddlers' convention at the local schoolhouse. He entered his first convention when he was eight years old and walked away with second prize. Grantham still lives near Eufaula, Alabama.

W.E. "CURLY" HANNAH was born 70 years ago in Blount County, Alabama. As a teenager, he began playing a Gibson banjo-mandolin, then took up the tenor banjo. He performed only in church until 1930, when he joined a group called the Midnight Ramblers, which played country music. He moved to Columbus, Georgia, in 1934 and organized a band called the Smoky Mountaineers, which played stage shows at schoolhouses and tobacco barns all over Georgia. These shows also featured a comedian and buck dancer. Today, he plays and sings only religious music at the church of God next door to his mobile home outside Phenix City, Alabama.

Born in 1914 in Talego, Georgia, **BESSIE HANNAH** sang in choirs as a child. She was the vocalist with the Smoky Mountaineers and was billed as "Shirley, the Sweetheart of the Barn Dance," on a popular country music show broadcast over WRBL Radio in Columbus. The Hannahs have been married 52 years.

JIMMY LEE HARRIS was born in 1935 in Seale, Alabama, about 10 miles from his present home of Phenix City. The first instrument he played was the mouthbow, which he made himself when he was nine. His parents bought him a guitar three years later, and he learned to play from a women named Seesa Vaughn. He and his brother Eddie, who lives in Columbus, still perform at occasional houseparties in the area.

H.L. "RED" HENLEY was born 57 years ago in Lee County, Alabama, where he lived until his death in May 1981. Henley, who is white, was taught to play harmonica by a black man. "He would blow it awhile," Henley recalled, "and then I would take it and wipe it on my shirt and blow it awhile." "Slow Buck" features Henley blowing the harp and buck dancing at the same time.

Born in 1927 in Coalfield, Tennessee, **GENE JACKSON** began playing fiddle at the age of eight, and was billed as a child prodigy in the family band. He was a professional musician until 1966, at which time he was forced out of the business on a fulltime basis by the lack of demand for his style of music. He has lived in Columbus since 1951 and plays with a bluegrass band every Friday night at a local barbecue establishment.

JOHN JAMES was born in 1930 in Carroll County, Mississippi. While he was in the Army he was stationed at Ft. Benning and, after marrying a Phenix City native, moved to Russell County, where he operates a country store.

MARION JONES was born in 1910 in Ellaville, Georgia. He learned to play fiddle at the age of 13 and two years later he and his three brothers formed a band that provided the music at square dances in the area.

ALBERT MACON lived in Macon County, Alabama, where he was born in 1920. He started blowing the harp when he was 10, learning to play the guitar from his father several years later. He played at "set frolics" (couples paid 10 cents a set to round dance) and at houseparties and schoolhouses. Macon and **ROBERT THOMAS**, 45, have been playing together for 20 years.

W.H. "BILL DAD" McGLAUN was born in 1922, 12 miles from Dothan, Alabama, where he currently resides. His first instrument was the harp; he began playing the guitar when he was 16. His mother, who was his major musical influence, played guitar, harp, and banjo. McGlaun did not start playing the fiddle until he was 22. "Me and some high school friends were getting up a band," he recalled. "They said, 'We need a fiddle player and you're it.' I thought they were joking, but they didn't crack a smile." McGlaun was nicknamed Bill Dad because it was more appropriate than McGlaun for the clown of the band, which McGlaun says every country music group was expected to have for stage shows. Since 1944, he has played professionally in the Dothan area.

Born in Meriwether County, Georgia, in 1928, **WALTER MEALOR** moved to Harris County in 1969. Like his father, Mealor is primarily a fiddler, but he also plays guitar, bass, and harp (his first instrument). His son **WARREN MEALOR**, who is 32 years old, plays guitar as well as banjo.

Several generations of the extended **MORRIS FAMILY** live in a rural community in Barbour county, Alabama, near Spring Hill. Members of the family formed a shape-note singing choir at Mt. Calvary Baptist Church in the 1920's, which has continued to flourish. Three of the choir's original members — Adolphus Morris, George Morris, and Annie Morris Hunter— still sing with the group. The other four singers are still all part of the Morris family, the youngest having joined the choir at the age of seven. There is a difference of 52 years between the oldest member, who is 80, and the youngest, who is 28.

Born in 1922, **WILLIAM ROBERTSON** was farmer all his life until he had to retire because of a back injury. Robertson began playing blues when he was five years old on a cooking oil can he had rigged up with a neck and one string. "Well, I left the cooking-oil can off and put me a wire upside of the house," he said, "and I played that with a bottleneck." Robertson began playing guitar when he was 12, and "started off ragging it, playing them tag pieces," which were traditional to the Chattahoochee Valley area.

CARTER RUSHING of Columbus, who was born in 1921 in Pike County, Alabama, remembers twin fiddling with his mother, who is still widely acknowledged as having been one of the best fiddle players in southern Alabama. In addition to the fiddle, he plays guitar and "sometimes harp when I'm possum hunting."

ROBERT SAXON, born in 1911 in Tennessee, began playing the pump organ before he was big enough to reach the pedals. By the age of seven, he was playing piano, his primary instrument today. He also learned to play most stringed instruments, and even constructed a couple of unique ones — a fiddle made from an axe handle and an oil funnel with a primitive electrical pickup and tenor banjo out of a Wesson oil can. After moving to Columbus in 1924, he began performing with bands in shows that also featured a black-faced comedian and tap dancer

"I watched my daddy's fingers on the guitar and I caught it," remembered **LONZIE THOMAS**, who was born in his present home of Lee county, Alabama, in 1921. He was shot in the face and blinded at the age of 22. "After I got blind, I got more interested in playing and singing," he said. "It was something to keep my mind off worrying." It was also one of the few ways a blind man could make a living, and he began playing on the streets of Opelika and Columbus for tips and at parties. Today, he plays occasionally for friends. **EDDIE B. HODGE** lives several miles up the road from Thomas, and for years the two have been musical buddies.

GEORGE MITCHELL
Summer , 1981

DISK 1

1. **FLAT FOOT FLOOGIE**
   Albert Macon, vocal and guitar; Robert Thomas, guitar

2. **DON'T NOTHING HURT ME BUT MY BACK AND SIDE**
   Albert Macon, vocal and guitar; Robert Thomas, guitar

3. **FLORIDA BLUES**
   Carter Rushing, fiddle; Robert George, guitar

4. **OLD JOE CLARK**
   Carter Rushing, fiddle and vocal; Robert George, guitar

5. **A LITTLE TOWN OF BIRMINGHAM**
   Robert Saxon, vocal and piano

6. **MOLLY DEAR**
   Robert Saxon, vocal and piano

7. **JACK OF DIAMONDS**
   William Grant, harmonica

8. **IT'S A GRAND AND GLORIOUS FEELING**
   The Morris Family

9. **DOWN YONDER**
   Marion Jones, fiddle

10. **HEN CACKLE**
    Marion Jones, fiddle

11. **SITTING HERE 1,000 MILES AWAY**
    Jimmy Lee Harris, vocal and guitar

12. **ALL NIGHT LONG**
    Jimmy Lee Harris, vocal and guitar

13. **SLOW BUCK**
    H.L. "Red" Henley, harmonica and buck dance; Oscar Whitlow, guitar

14. **I'VE BEEN TREATED SO BAD**
    Cliff Davis, vocal

15. **WHEN THE BLUEBIRD SINGS**
    Joe Berry, vocal and guitar; Doug Booth, vocal and guitar; Wendell Berry, bass

16. **COLUMBUS STOCKADE BLUES**
    Joe Berry, vocal and guitar; Doug Booth, fiddle and vocal; Wendell Berry, bass

17. **HOME SWEET HOME**
    Warren Mealor, banjo; Walter Mealor, guitar

DISK 2

1. **LONZIE THOMAS DRAGAROUND**
   Lonzie Thomas, vocal and guitar

2. **RED CROSS STORE**
   Lonzie Thomas, vocal and guitar

3. **ORANGE BLOCCOM SPECIAL**
   W.H. "Bill Dad" McGlaun, fiddle; Royce McKee, guitar

4. **WHEN THE SAINTS GO MARCHING IN**
   Precious Bryant, vocal and guitar

5. **GEORGIA BUCK**
   Precious Bryant, guitar

6. **JIMMY BROWN AND THE NEWSBOY**
   John James, vocal and guitar

7. **BLUE YODEL**
   John James, vocal and guitar

8. **CITY OF GOLD**
   Bessie Hannah, vocal and piano; W.E. Hannah, tenor banjo

9. **BEAR CREEK HOP**
   Comer Grantham, fiddle; Norwood Hall and Mack McHan, guitar

10. **ROCK OF AGES**
    Doug Booth, vocal and guitar; Joe Berry, guitar; Wendell Berry, bass

11. **HELLO, STRANGER**
    Doug Booth, vocal and guitar; Joe Berry, guitar; Wendell Berry, bass

12. **TRUE LOVE**
    William Robertson, vocal and guitar

13. **LONESOME HOUSE BLUES**
    William Robertson, vocal and guitar

14. **ALABAMA GIRL**
    Alfred Dickerson, banjo; Barney Dickerson, fiddle; Doyle Dickerson and Luther Hasty, guitars

15. **BABY, PLEASE DON'T GO**
    Eddie B. Hodge, vocal and guitar

16. **BLACKBERRY BLOSSOM**
    Gene Jackson, fiddle; Doug Martin, guitar

17. **HOUSE OF DAVID BLUES**
    Gene Jackson, fiddle; Doug Martin, guitar

18. **HAMBONE**
    Ray Favors